CREATING POLITICAL ORDER

CREATING POLITICAL ORDER

The Party-States of West Africa

Aristide R. Zolberg

The University of Chicago Press
Chicago and London

The University of Chicago Press, Chicago 60637
The University of Chicago Press, Ltd., London
© 1966 by Aristide R. Zolberg
Midway reprint 1985
All rights reserved. Published 1985
Printed in the United States of America
ISBN: 0-226-98901-1

ACKNOWLEDGMENTS

As a critical work this book often questions statements, observations, and hypotheses advanced by distinguished scholars in the field of African political studies. Lest this be misunderstood by readers not yet fully involved in the scholarly life, I should like to dispel any impression that I am attempting in this way to minimize the contributions of other Africanists, some of whom were my teachers, and most of whom are now friends and colleagues. If some of the ideas and suggestions contained in this book are stimulating and sound, it is due especially to the pioneering work of those whom I sometimes take to task and to whom I am therefore particularly grateful.

The writing of this short book has spanned four years of intermittent activity since it was initiated in mid-1961 at the suggestion of Professor Myron Weiner. During the first two of those years I profited from the stimulating presence of many colleagues in the Department of Political Science at the University of Wisconsin, and received some research assistance from that University. Since the summer of 1963 I have benefited from the financial and intellectual aid generously given by the Department of Political Science, the Committee for the Comparative Study of New Nations (itself supported by the Carnegie Corporation of New York), and the Divisional Social Science Research Council at the University of Chicago. Most of 1964 was spent doing research in Africa with the assistance of a grant from the African Studies Committee of the Social Science Research Council (joint with the American Council of Learned Societies); some of the preliminary results of this research are included here. During that year I benefited from exchange with other itinerant or resident scholars in West Africa, particularly William Jones, Martin Klein, Thomas Hodgkin, and Ernst Benjamin; while spending three months at Makerere College, University of East Africa, I had further discussions with colleagues and friends, especially Colin Leys, Ali Mazrui, Geoffrey Engholm, and

Henry Bienen; everywhere in Africa, friends and officials extended their hospitality. Some of the ideas in this book were included in a paper presented at the 1964 meetings of the American Political Science Association, and I am grateful to the panel chairman, John Lewis, for having given me the opportunity to pull these thoughts together publicly. Professors Rupert Emerson, David Greenstone, David Easton, William Foltz, and Jan Vansina applied their critical minds to the final manuscript and helped me clarify and correct many points. Throughout this period several research assistants helped with the ungrateful task of assembling piecemeal materials: they include especially Arezki Hammoun, Larry Bowman, William Kornblum, and Linda Wortman. My wife and daughter helped most of all by being themselves in spite of many discomforts.

If it appears that this mountain of aid, encouragement, and stimulation has given birth to a very small mouse, it is solely because of my own deficiencies as an obstetrician.

A. R. Z.

TABLE OF CONTENTS

	Acknowledgments	v
	Introduction	1
I	The Emergence of Dominant Parties	19
II	The One-Party Ideology	37
III	The Achievement of Unanimity	66
IV	The Creation of a New Institutional Order	93
V	The Party-State in Perspective	128
	Conclusions	151
	Index	163

INTRODUCTION

IT WAS ONLY IN THE MID-1950'S, WHEN THE BEACON OF INDEPENDENCE was lit at the end of the Gold Coast's constitutional path, that observers of African politics, who had been wondering whether what was happening on the continent could properly be labeled "nationalism" and whether dependent territories were ready for self-government, began to speculate about the character of the nascent regimes. Some expressed concern over the appearance of a host of powerless and possibly racially embittered new nations on the world scene and raised as a danger flag their doubtful international orientation. Most political scientists who were in the field sufficiently early to share in the enthusiasm of the new men at the helm of the liberating movements, however, were caught up in the drama of man's search for polity which was being re-enacted in a new and strange environment. The study of African politics provided a great and exciting intellectual adventure comparable to the quests which earlier had driven explorers to overcome apparently insurmountable obstacles on the same continent. These intrepid men no longer sought to trace the sources of the Nile or the course of the Niger. The new challenge was to discover, with the help of imaginative theories of society, a system of rivulets which might merge into a new stream of democracy.

While to the general public at this time African politics suggested little more than the occasional headlines about Mau-Mau in Kenya, serious students had great expectations for West Africa, where as early as 1951, the dignified Governor of the Gold Coast had brought a gallant American-educated nationalist leader out of prison and asked him to become Leader of Government Business. For some, the photographs of a miniature tropical Westminster presided over by a bewigged speaker simply provided an occasion for Waugh-like irony; for others such images were but the surface expression of a unique experiment in African self-government. When the Gold Coast became independent in 1957, the event was greeted in much of the American press as a triumph of ancient Wilsonian ideals. Ghana was now the exemplar. Even the most sympathetic observers, however, soon began to discern political patterns which indicated that liberation from foreign rule might not coincide with the birth of democracy. The government of Ghana severely restricted the freedom of its opponents and increasingly appeared to forget the British model as successfully as students everywhere forget their book learning when its leaders stressed that a country could develop only if ruled by a single political party. When in later years the Ghanaians added to this a Socialist orientation and vociferous attacks on imperialism and neo-colonialism, although American attitudes toward Ghana did not reverse as sharply as did those toward Cuba during the same period, Ghana came to be viewed first as an irritating little country and then increasingly as a dangerous one.

Meanwhile, new countries were being born. The American public knew much less about Guinea in 1958, but those who followed current events in that part of the world were torn between sympathy for a country which had dared defy De Gaulle and suspicion of the Jacobin virtue exhibited by some of its leaders who proudly announced that henceforth thieves would be shot. The crucial year was 1960. Ghana became a republic and resorted to a government-controlled plebiscite to elect its first President. Among the remaining countries of French-speaking Africa for whom strange name cards were placed at international conference tables that year, the one-party regime was the usual pattern, regardless of how these countries were prepared to vote in the General Assembly of the United Nations. Democratic hopes rose with Nigeria, but fell to a new low with the Congo.

The realization that most new states were brought to life as one-party regimes has been a source of concern for American students of politics because in its most common form democratic theory rests on the competitive model of the late Joseph Schumpeter and on a long tradition of pluralist thought.[1] Many believe that "one might recognize in the opposition of the one party versus the two and multi-parties the fundamental cleavage of our time: dictatorship versus democracy."[2] Once it was replied that "at this stage of West African party history

[1] Joseph A. Schumpeter, *Capitalism, Socialism and Democracy* (3d ed.; New York: Harper and Brothers, 1950), p. 269.
[2] Sigmund Neumann (ed.), *Modern Political Parties* (Chicago: University of Chicago Press, 1956), p. 403.

... the number of parties is far too simple a criterion upon which to decide whether or not a system is democratic," the debate was on.³ While the birth of new states in Africa progressed arithmetically, commentaries have accumulated at a geometric rate. They rapidly spilled over from the specialized journals and monographs to innumerable academic conferences, expensive ad hoc international congresses, and into a host of publications ranging from the precious pages of *Encounter* or *Commentary* to the robust records of congressional subcommittees. Sociologists and anthropologists joined political scientists and journalists in the fray. In recent years, no program chairman or editor has rested without having decreed "let there be light" on this issue.

* * *

Much of the debate can be viewed as a quarrel between optimists and pessimists whose divergent inclinations lead them to perceive reality differently and to reach almost diametrically opposed conclusions. The soundest arguments in the optimistic view have rested less on the appearance of democratic constitutions than on the functions of nationalist leaders and movements from the point of view of the entire society. For example, David Apter viewed pre-independence Gold Coast unambiguously as "an area marked by singular success in the transformation from a tribal dependency to a parliamentary democracy . . ."⁴ and concentrated his efforts on applying social theory to an understanding of how this transition occurred, selecting leadership as the catalyst and the mass party, the Convention People's Party (CPP), as the crucible in which new norms and new relationships, compatible with parliamentary democracy, were being formed. These two aspects of the system also held the key to the future. Discussing "The Prospects of Gold Coast Democracy" in his concluding chapter, he was clearly more worried about the consequences of the weakening of charisma, the "integrative integer," than with its potential use as a steppingstone toward autocracy. As for the party, he recognized a major danger but doubted its realization: "The authoritarian potential of the CPP remains unknown. There is little reason to feel that it will do other than remain latent unless the entire regime is threatened

---

³Ruth Schachter [Morgenthau], "Single-Party Systems in West Africa," *The American Political Science Review*, LV, No. 2 (June, 1961), 294.

⁴David Apter, *The Gold Coast in Transition* (Princeton: Princeton University Press, 1955), p. vii.

by disorder and local rebellions."⁵ Soon after the book in which these remarks were written was published, the rulers of Ghana had come to believe in the reality of such threats and, in keeping with Apter's hypothesis, the regime had begun to react to growing insecurity by deviating from the parliamentary path.

Henry Bretton, who looked at Ghana at about this time, launched a diatribe against Apter's alleged lack of realism and wishful thinking:

> David Apter, for some reason expecting parliamentary democracy to develop in the Gold Coast, given certain conditions, bases upon this expectation an elaborate theory of institutional transfer. His utilization of advanced sociological principles to the Gold Coast lends the experiment there—it is no more than that—an unwarranted appearance of respectability and permanence.⁶

Bretton's might be taken as representative of the pessimistic view, stemming from a flair for detecting evil beneath the most attractive political surface, which behooves a former student of German politics. Selecting the same materials for emphasis as Apter—the role of Kwame Nkrumah, the structure of the party, and the political thought of the new leaders—he concluded that the transition would not stop at parliamentary democracy. This stage "in turn, by the premature application of universal franchise, might be followed by a pronounced non-democratic, in all probability authoritarian-totalitarian movement" which might be "not only of the Marxist, but also of the fascist variety" although perhaps in a modified form "making allowance for organizational deficiencies."⁷

A year after Bretton's visit, Apter returned to Ghana. He now stressed the CPP's fundamentally ambiguous character more clearly than before: "The party remains characteristically open and fraternal. But it tends to identify with its own creation, Ghana, and to remain outside the embrace of the party is to be suspect."⁸ Although institutional transfer of *parliamentary* democracy had not occurred and the future remained uncertain, his over-all judgment about the present

---

⁵*Ibid.*, p. 316.
⁶Henry L. Bretton, "Current Political Thought and Practice in Ghana," *The American Political Science Review*, LII (March, 1958), 48.
⁷*Ibid.*, pp. 49, 50, 57.
⁸See Apter's preface to the second printing of *The Gold Coast in Transition* (1959), p. xiii. Apter's further reappraisal is contained in the preface and final chapter of *Ghana in Transition* (New York: Athenaeum, 1963).

remained firm: "Ghana is, for all intents and purposes, a one-party democracy."⁹ This concept of "one-party democracy" was not a mere debater's trick. It implied a distinction between one-party systems striving for total control of the society and regimes in which one party was dominant but exercised a substantial degree of self-restraint in the form of respect for the rule of law, for certain forms of opposition, and for free associational life. The latter type fell into the category of "tutelary democracy" provided by Edward Shils and could understandably be viewed as the best regime that one might hope for in a new, underdeveloped nation.¹⁰ Many of the optimists went beyond this, however, and suggested that a regime of this type provides a democratic sector within a transitional society and that this sector will be enlarged through the functional consequences of the regime's activities.¹¹ The pessimists believe instead that the African one-party state is an imperfect form of totalitarianism only for technical reasons and that it will be transformed into a full-fledged totalitarian state over time.

After nearly a decade of this, the thoughtful student of comparative politics might well conclude with what an eminent student of comparative anatomy said about an issue in his own field: "'It is a highly debatable problem'—that is to say, one with so little evidence to its credit that no debate is in reality worth while."¹² But he then went on to review the evidence that was available and attempted to provide new guidelines for research. I shall follow suit.

* * *

A most significant aspect of the debate is that most of the participants have seized upon the internal structure of the dominant party and the organization's relationship to society as the most significant data. Most projections rest on this foundation. But how firm is it empirically? Its inadequacies are most clearly visible in the difficulties which *both* optimists and pessimists have encountered in coming to grips with the appearance of endemic disorder on the African political

---

⁹*Ibid.*

¹⁰Edward Shils, "Political Development in the New States," *Comparative Studies in Society and History*, II, No. 4 (June, 1960), 389–93.

¹¹See Morgenthau, *op. cit.*, and the works of Hodgkin and Wallerstein discussed in Chapter I.

¹²P. B. Medawar, *The Uniqueness of the Individual* (London: Methuen and Co., 1957), p. 32.

scene. The year of birth of most one-party states was also, as we have seen, that of the Congo. It was rapidly evident that here the danger stemming from an absence of authority was clearly greater than that of too much power. But the Congo has usually been analyzed as a case *sui generis* and its difficulties attributed to the especially unfortunate circumstances of the decolonization process. Is it truly unique? No sooner had the notion of "one-party system" been singled out as a most important classificatory concept than some of them appeared to vacillate under the blows of internecine rivalries among the ruling elite, ethnic rebellions, military coups, or social and intergenerational conflict. When African leaders began to react by voicing their fears and tightening their hold, their behavior was often stigmatized as pathological. But is it not possible that these superficially strong men are more deeply aware than most observers of the structural weaknesses of their regimes?[13]

We have thus reached an impasse. There is still talk about totalitarian trends as well as about the democratic potential of one-party states, but the dramatic danger of disorder and the less spectacular but clear and present danger of stagnation and perhaps even of regression impose themselves on our attention. Does Africa suffer from too much authority or from too little authority? Surely this is a prior question which lifts the study of the politics of one-party states in Africa above the level of contemporary headlines and links it to fundamental issues well within the mainstream of past and present concerns of political science.

When we seek to elucidate this question by examining the structure and process of African political systems, we realize that in spite of the huge growth of scholarly and popular literature, our information is grossly deficient. Much has been written about the thought of various leaders in the fields of international politics, about economic development, and about the one-party state itself. We know what political organizations *say* their structure is like and what they *say* concerning their operations, but we have seldom gone beyond such declaratory statements. Our knowledge about most countries where "one-party systems" exist is extremely limited because the number of reliable monographs remains pitifully small. It is therefore impossible

---

[13]The fall of Kwame Nkrumah in February, 1966, occurred while this book was in press. Since this event appears to support the major propositions and interpretations it contains, I have not made any changes in the text. I hope the reader will simply substitute the past tense for the present wherever necessary.

at this time to state a reliable set of propositions about "one-party systems" in general.

Hence, the objectives of this book are consciously limited to an examination of certain aspects of political life in five countries about which I have been able to acquire a reasonable level of information. I visited the Ivory Coast and Mali several times between 1959 and 1964 and conducted extensive field work in both countries. For Ghana I have had the benefit of many studies conducted by outstanding scholars and other visitors at different times; in addition, I spent brief periods there in 1959 and 1964. Although Senegal and Guinea have been included because of the intrinsic interest of these countries, I have had to rely, in regard to them, almost exclusively on a few excellent monographs and on much less reliable press reports. The five countries selected represent the two major colonial legacies in West Africa, and they vary a great deal in terms of culture and general level of socio-economic development. Although they are all "one-party states," they have somewhat different orientations on certain issues; some writers have distinguished among them between "pragmatic-pluralist" and "revolutionary-centralizing" regimes.[14] All these differences are important because they enhance striking and perhaps unexpected similarities in the patterns of post-independence politics visible in all five countries. I believe that these similarities are fundamental and that "the West African party-state" is a useful typological term. What I hope to provide is not so much a series of scientific propositions about this type of system but an analytic description of the type.

The organization of the chapters reflects some methodological assumptions and practical considerations. Initially it is necessary to review how dominant parties emerged in West Africa in order to appreciate what might be called the "structural inheritance" of the new states; Chapter I, which fulfills this purpose, also provides the necessary historical background for the rest of the study. The transformation of colonial territories into new nations is a crucial phenomenon which is considered in Chapter II from one particular point of view, the changing outlook of the leadership. It is a chapter on "ideology," using this concept in a very broad sense, which is particularly warranted because the leadership have been in a position to act in

---

[14] See, especially, James S. Coleman and Carl G. Rosberg, Jr., *Political Parties and National Integration in Tropical Africa* (Berkeley and Los Angeles: University of California Press, 1964). These distinctions will be discussed in Chapter IV.

INTRODUCTION

accordance with their beliefs. How they have translated these beliefs into political action will be considered in two chapters: first, Chapter III on obstacles to their authority and their dealings with opponents; and second, Chapter IV on the construction of instruments of rule. In Chapter V, I shall return to the broader concerns raised in this introduction and suggest that we must view these regimes in perspective—the perspective of time, the perspective of the society in which they operate, and finally the perspective of the universe of political systems.

The final chapter contains two sets of conclusions. The first consists of some suggestions for future research—the academic conclusion; but in the second I shall discuss the one-party state from the point of view of its own members—a conclusion addressed to the African friends to whom this book is dedicated.

CHAPTER I

THE EMERGENCE OF DOMINANT PARTIES

CURRENT CONCEPTS

IN THE LITERATURE ON AFRICAN POLITICS, THE EMERGENCE OF A DOMINANT organization appears to have been almost inevitable in the countries where it occurred because of the organization's greater political fitness. This conclusion can be attributed in part to the fact that the political history of Africa tends to be written from the point of view of the winners. When scholars went to the field, the outcome of political competition had become fairly clear. It was therefore natural for them to concentrate on the most important organization. Since they depended for their work on information which could be properly annotated, it was equally natural to learn more about political groups which were more self-conscious about organization than about those which were not. The former held congresses more regularly, printed manifestoes, and had headquarters and sometimes even a permanent staff—however small—where one could acquire organizational charts, party constitutions, and other concrete evidence, while the others usually did not. Although later, after the one-party systems had been established, interest in what were by then "opposition" groups grew, it became very difficult to gain access to them and to reconstruct the past except through the eyes of the rulers. Hence, the genuine structural differences that did exist among these various groups tended to be exaggerated once they had been sifted through the observer's and the participant's perceptual apparatus.

This exaggeration underlies the classification of political órganizations provided by Hodgkin and Morgenthau in the course of their otherwise excellent pioneer works on West African politics. Morgenthau, for example, drew a sharp contrast between "mass" parties on the one hand, and "cadre" or "patron" parties on the other. Mass parties claim to represent all the people, tend to have either institutional or personal leadership, are strongly articulated, relatively disciplined, use organization as a weapon, are led by more educated men, legitimize formal structures of government and integrate the population into a nation, and are moving toward democracy. Patron parties have personal leadership, are weakly articulated, comparatively undisciplined, have little direct membership participation, tend to be based on "native authorities," do not integrate the population, and are not democratic.[1] Hodgkin subscribes to the same distinctions between "mass" and "elite" parties, but reduces them to one fundamental difference: "To state the contrast in the simplest form, elite parties are content to reflect the structure of society as it is, or as it used to be; while mass parties attempt to impose their own new type of structure upon society."[2] For him as for Morgenthau, "the mass parties . . . are organisms of a more highly evolved type . . . . In the internal struggle for power which develops during the period of decolonization, elite parties tend therefore to lose ground to mass parties."[3]

However useful this basic classification was in clearing the underbrush, it has created some serious difficulties. First, by attributing the success of certain movements almost exclusively to their structural characteristics, it has tended to overly magnify the contrast between them and their opponents. Second, the nature of their success must be specified more carefully if the difficulties they encountered after independence are to become clear. Third, perhaps because of circumstances beyond the control of the originators of the concept, the notion of "mass" party carries some connotations which are not applicable to West Africa. There is no doubt that many of the organizations which fall into this category have long *aspired* to resemble parties of the European left described by Duverger; but whether they have successfully achieved more than a surface resemblance to their models is another question altogether, one which requires a careful re-examination of the manner in which they grew.

A further problem arises when such general observations are invested with a statistical regularity—without specifying the conditions

---

[1] Ruth Schachter [Morgenthau], "Single-Party Systems in West Africa," *The American Political Science Review*, LV, No. 2 (June, 1961), *passim*. The distinction owes much to Duverger's classification in *Political Parties* (New York: John Wiley & Sons, 1954), esp. pp. 63–71.

[2] Thomas Hodgkin, *African Political Parties* (Harmondsworth: Penguin Books, 1961), p. 69.

[3] *Ibid.*, p. 70.

under which it occurs—and then deviant cases are classified into a sort of pathological category. Wallerstein, for example, begins a discussion of the subject by stating that

> most African nations came to independence by organizing a nationalist movement which laid effective claim to power. The standard pattern was the existence of one major party, which symbolized the struggle for independence, with some weak, often regionalist opposition parties. . . . Where there was no one party which commanded overwhelming support . . . there often was considerable trouble.[4]

These two patterns then become predictive, as the same writer continues,

> Almost everywhere, the trend after independence has been in one of two directions: toward a one-party state with consequent stability (if the resulting single party grouped the major elements) or toward a breakdown of the party system with consequent instability.[5]

The parenthetical qualification, together with the clause "which commanded overwhelming support" in the preceding quotation, provides a clue to the problem with such statements: they anticipate the possibility of instability by making it possible to argue in retrospect that such an outcome would be proof that the organizations involved were not genuine "single parties" of the proper type to start with. Hence, if we want to have a sound understanding of the political process in these states, we must understand the characteristics of the dominant parties *before* the consequences of their operations become clear.

A further difficulty is that such statements often act as the bridge to arguments about desirability of the outcome. Given the above generalizations, Wallerstein concludes that "the choice has not been between one-party and multi-party states; it has been between one-party states and either anarchy or military regimes or various combinations of the two."[6] The implication is clearly that any reasonable man will bow to historical necessity. But whether we choose to do so or not, we would presumably want to be sure of the soundness of this

---

[4]Immanuel Wallerstein, *Africa: The Politics of Independence* (New York: Vintage Books, 1961), p. 95.
[5]*Ibid.*
[6]*Ibid.*

entire interpretation. It is with this goal in mind that we shall review briefly a decade of political history.

THE INITIAL SPURT

Among the many groups which appeared in West Africa shortly after World War II were some headed by leaders who were better able than other men to capture the spirit of widespread aspirations, who were quicker than others to learn the value of organization and of communications, who were willing to engage in mass action, and who were bolder in attacking the status quo defined by the colonial administration. Although it is always puzzling, in retracing the life history of movements, to account for individual differences, we are not concerned here with the sources of this phenomenon but rather with its consequences. Some individuals had acquired their set of concepts about political ends and appropriate means through their own study and experience abroad, as Nkrumah, for example, indicates in his autobiography; others benefited from the presence of sympathetic and experienced advisers, as was the case for many of the founders of the *Rassemblement Démocratique African* (RDA) and of other parties in French-speaking Africa, where French Socialists and Communists acted as technical advisers.

Previously, there had been Africans who had become spokesmen for shared grievances, but they had usually been chiefs and other notabilities co-opted into colonial councils, individuals chosen by very small electorates in municipalities, legal-minded men who had mastered the arts of petition and of journalistic discussion, but who were unable or unwilling to engage in the more vulgar aspects of mass politics. There had also been some mass movements, such as messianic cults and independent churches, but on the whole these arose too early. The new leaders benefited from two major changes in the political situation. First, the many cultural, social, and economic changes that began during the 1920's were accelerated by the effects of World War II and its aftermath; they resulted in a growing stratum of "transitionals," individuals no longer fully in the traditional society but not yet modern, who were available for mobilization.[7] For the older generation of nationalists, they constituted an uncouth mass which jeopardized the hard-earned respectability a few Africans had

---

[7] For these concepts see Daniel Lerner, *The Passing of Traditional Society* (Glencoe, Ill.: The Free Press, 1958).

acquired in European eyes; for the new organization-minded politicians, they were a reservoir of immense potential strength. Second, along with a revolution in the international situation World War II brought a major reorientation of domestic politics in France and Britain, and a fundamental change in the colonial outlook.[8] Although the reforms often did not go as far as politically-conscious Africans desired, there was a new willingness to allow some Africans at least to participate in the government of their territories. However reluctantly it was conceded, sooner or later—in French-speaking West Africa from 1945 on, in Ghana in 1950—this meant elections.

The new wave accomplished its initial aim with very meager means. They used bicycles, a few trucks, or very occasionally an automobile. They sometimes had some private funds, but relied mainly upon a small band of dedicated men. The organizations they created were at first very limited: some form of executive composed of the co-founders, a larger group of correspondents with contacts among various voluntary associations, mainly in the capital and a few key towns in the hinterland, and among various ethnic groups. The organizations were centered in the capital and extended to a handful of branches in the hinterland. They did not ask for much: most important of all, a willingness to agitate in the marketplace, to greet vociferously a passing European official, sometimes the payment of a small membership fee in exchange for the promise that grievances would be set right and of a place in the new society, and very soon afterwards, a vote. They channeled the agitation which prevailed almost everywhere in West Africa in the tumultuous postwar years. This unrest stemmed not only from specific political grievances, but also from a variety of unrelated causes such as shortages and high prices of imported consumer goods, fluctuation in the prices farmers obtained for their cash crops, impatience with the chiefs, low wages, and bad housing conditions. By providing rallying symbols and banners, by personalizing the struggle, these small organizations became the spearheads of movements.

Few reliable observers have reported on the organization of the party at that time and it is extremely difficult to reconstruct it in retrospect. Austin points out that at the time it won its first major victory (1951), the Convention People's Party (CPP) had had little time to organize. How the victory was won

---

[8] The effects of World War II on colonial areas are discussed by Rupert Emerson in *From Empire to Nation* (Cambridge: Harvard University Press, 1960), pp. 22–36.

... was something of a mystery even to its organizers. Its appeal to the "Common Man" and for "Self-Government Now" ran like a flame through the Colony and Ashanti chiefdoms and branches were formed in many instances without the knowledge of the national headquarters.[9]

Leadership during this period was essentially collective and "the nationalist party was still inchoate in 1951."[10] The party's formal constitution, setting up a pyramid with branches at the bottom, an annual National Conference which also included affiliates (women, youth, etc.), a national executive committee with its inner central committee headed by the Leader, had been written at the founding in 1949 and was approved formally in 1951, *after* the elections. But, Austin warns, this formal structure "bore as little relation to the way in which the party worked in practice as most constitutions do to the parties they purport to describe."[11] This corresponds to my own retrospective portrait of the *Parti Démocratique de Côte d'Ivoire* (PDCI) during the 1946–51 period, when initially "The founders of the P.D.C.I. forged unity out of an amalgam of heterogeneous components by constructing an indirect party in which individuals were not members of the party but of social groups that belonged to the party,"[12] and afterwards, in spite of attempts to transform it into a highly disciplined organization, "party officials, working under the fire of the colonial authorities, sacrificed organizational theory to effectiveness. The result was a different kind of organization altogether."[13]

Such rudimentary structures were sufficient because these organizations had the immense advantage of moving into what was almost an organizational vacuum. The transitionals to whom these efforts were directed were in Kornhauser's terms, "available non-elites."[14] The situation comes close to fitting the model he had in mind: "In the absence of proximate sources of gratification and restraint, individuals may become highly responsive to the appeal of mass movements bent on

---

[9]Dennis Austin, *Politics in Ghana* (London: Oxford University Press, 1964), p. 114.
[10]*Ibid.*, p. 163.
[11]*Ibid.*
[12]*One-Party Government in the Ivory Coast* (Princeton: Princeton University Press, 1964), p. 76.
[13]*Ibid.*, p. 116.
[14]William Kornhauser, *The Politics of Mass Society* (New York: The Free Press of Glencoe, 1959), pp. 60 ff.

the transformation of the world."¹⁵ That these leaders were the first to establish a relationship between individuals and an organization gave them a very great advantage over those who came along later, since the latter had either to try to reach individuals who were less reachable or to undo what the initial organization had done.

For the three countries where the first organization of this type to emerge was successful from the very beginning, it is possible to specify how far they were carried by the impetus of their initial spurt of activity. In the Ivory Coast, the Houphouet-Boigny organization obtained 94 per cent of the votes cast in the December, 1946, elections to the territorial assembly (a total of 67,874).[16] This is a good measure of its superiority over its opponents, but it gives us little information about support for the movement as a whole in a country of about two and a half million people. The votes it gained amounted to 53 per cent of the eligible electorate who had registered, but since the electorate was a very restricted one, these votes represented only about 6 per cent of the estimated adult population. In 1950-51, when the PDCI was being fought by the colonial administration, it claimed nearly one million members—approximately two-thirds of the entire adult population. But in the 1952 election, which the leaders acknowledge to be fair, when the party won a great victory over its opponents, who obtained only 28 per cent of the votes cast, its total number of votes was about the same as it had been in 1946 but it represented only 33 per cent of the enlarged electorate.

In Ghana the first test of the CPP's territorial strength came in the 1951 elections, two years after its founding. The CPP's victory was overwhelming: it obtained 92 per cent of the votes cast in Accra and 94 per cent of those cast in the other municipalities, where elections were direct.[17] In addition, it obtained 72 per cent of votes cast by grand electors in the rural areas of the administrative regions then called the Colony and Ashanti. What did these results indicate in terms of overall support? In the five municipalities, 64 per cent of the qualified population registered to vote; of these, 47.2 per cent voted. Hence, the voters represented about 30 per cent of the eligible population, itself somewhat smaller than the total number of adults. Hence, the CPP's

---

[15] *Ibid.*, p. 61.
[16] All electoral figures for the Ivory Coast were drawn from my earlier book and re-analyzed for the present purpose.
[17] Unless otherwise indicated, all electoral figures for Ghana were drawn from Austin; the breakdown in percentages and the interpretation are my own.

performance in the cities indicates that it was able to elicit a positive indication of support from about one-fifth to one-fourth of the adult population, a startling achievement for a party that had been founded just two years earlier and many of whose leaders had been in jail during the campaign. But this result cannot be taken as an indication of territorial saturation by the CPP. As Austin put it, with the benefit of hindsight,

> It was . . . easy to be misled by the sweeping success of the C.P.P. in the February elections into supposing that the party was fully in control of the country. . . . Although the C.P.P. leaders had been remarkably successful in making articulate a general dissatisfaction with colonial rule, they were to find it a far more difficult task to keep this discontent within bounds, and prevent it from being turned against themselves.[18]

In Senegal, Leopold Senghor organized the first mass-oriented party in 1948, at a time when earlier groups were unable or unwilling to extend their grasp beyond the municipalities. Like its predecessors, the *Bloc Démocratique Sénégalais* was initially modeled after the Socialist (SFIO) party of France, but later increasingly incorporated African characteristics. According to Robinson, around 1951–52 it was in theory less highly articulated than the PDCI of the Ivory Coast and other RDA sections which had been inspired by a Communist model, but very much like them in practice. Its branches were often led by notabilities in major towns and the party managed to weld a variety of ethnic groups and kinship-political groupings usually called "clans" (not in the strict anthropological sense) in the Senegalese political jargon.[19] In spite of its relative looseness, the party met its first major test with great success, securing 68 per cent of the votes cast in the 1951 elections, or about one-third of the registered electorate and perhaps 10 to 15 per cent of the adult Senegalese population; this performance was repeated in 1952.

These illustrations tell us more about the weakness of other groups than about the strength of the mass movements, and they demonstrate that during the initial political phase even a slight structural increment

---

[18]Austin, p. 154.
[19]Kenneth Robinson, "Political Developments in French West Africa," in Calvin W. Stillman (ed.), *Africa in the Modern World* (Chicago: University of Chicago Press, 1955), pp. 177–78.

could bring very great marginal returns. Beyond the winning of elections, these usually included recognition by the colonial authorities. In this respect, an interesting process was at work. Although officials initially attempted to belittle the importance and the representativeness of the mass movements, they were often faced with recurrent disruptions of law and order; since it would be humiliating to report that they could not cope with run-of-the-mill disturbances in their district, they suggested that such events were the result of a highly organized challenge to their own authority. In the process, of course, the reputations of the movements and of their leaders were greatly enhanced in the eyes of both Europeans and Africans. Furthermore, after the initial period of conflict, when the time came to sit down at the bargaining table to negotiate the next step in constitutional evolution or in reform, on one side of the table there had to be a spokesman for the African collectivity. With relatively few exceptions, the leaders of troublesome mass-oriented organizations were accepted in this role of *interlocuteur valable*. The classic case in West Africa was that of Ghana. In retrospect, Sir Charles Arden-Clarke, Governor of the Gold Coast, who brought Kwame Nkrumah out of prison in 1951 to ask him to become Leader of Government Business, stated: "Nkrumah and his party had the mass of the people behind them and there was no other party with appreciable public support to which we could turn."[20] In the same year, after repeated efforts to destroy the PDCI and to promote other political groups, the administration of the Ivory Coast came to terms with Houphouet-Boigny and even went so far as to abandon its own political creatures.

One might think that the willingness of such leaders to cooperate with the colonial power after the first major victory might be interpreted as a sell-out that would cost them popular support. But the fact that rather the opposite took place suggests another advantage which accrued to the victorious mass movement. Within two years of the founding of the CPP, Nkrumah was Leader of Government Business in the Gold Coast; within an even shorter span of time, Houphouet-Boigny in the Ivory Coast, Senghor in Senegal, and others had become members of the French parliament. To whatever charisma they possessed in the eyes of their followers was added the charisma of European power. The African view that Europeans possessed special gifts was commonly encountered throughout much of the continent; it was

---

[20] Quoted by Austin, p. 150.

advanced by Mannoni as a hypothesis to explain Malagasy political behavior, and explored by Jahoda in regard to Ghana. There, among individuals with very little education and little contact with whites, he suggested that

> the ordinary member of a village community will not only accept the distant authority of the whites, but will come to regard their position as an essential part of the order of the universe, on which his own life and security rest. It is thus more than a mere relationship of dominance and submission, being at the same time less direct . . . and more deep-seated."[21]

This Jahoda relates to the "natural priestliness" of Europeans in the eyes of many Africans.[22]

It is likely that this respect was transferred to the Africans who assumed the roles hitherto filled by Europeans: a prime minister or *député* was like a governor, a representative to the territorial council like a district commissioner or a *commandant*. This could even occur *before* a leader formally occupied such a role. In Guinea, for example, one year after the French administration had engineered the electoral defeat of Sékou Touré, the other RDA leaders who already held high office deliberately chose Conakry for a meeting of their coordinating committee. The Minister of Overseas France and the Governor-General of French West Africa, by then anxious to conciliate African politicians, attended a vast parade held for the occasion. According to Ruth Morgenthau, "there were not enough seats when Sékou Touré and his wife arrived. The Minister and the Governor-General offered their chairs." Soon afterwards, people were singing in the streets "that in Conakry, Sékou is Governor," and that "Sékou says he is not a chief, but today they wisely gave him power." [23] It may well be that the symbolic seat occupied by Sékou Touré that day contributed to his rapid rise as a national personality in the months that followed, culminating in his electoral victory the following year.

A more immediately tangible consequence of initial victory was

---

[21]Gustav Jahoda, *White Man, A Study of the Attitudes of Africans to Europeans in Ghana Before Independence* (London: Oxford University Press, 1961), p. 111. See also O. Mannoni, *Prospero and Caliban* (New York: Praeger, 1956).

[22]Jahoda, pp. 77, 111.

[23]Ruth Morgenthau, *Political Parties in French-Speaking West Africa* (London: Oxford University Press, 1964), p. 242.

the access it gave to well-paid political offices and to participation in the allocation of benefits. Since 1951 the CPP has controlled for practical purposes a rather large budget and has been able to determine where schools or roads will be built, who will get government loans, and who will be appointed to a variety of public boards, much as in an American city. Although this did not occur formally in French-speaking Africa until 1957, long before this, leading politicians who operated in the French parliament were able to exert a similar sort of leverage on the government of their territories. To their other advantages the movements were able to add those which accrue to any political machine operating in a society where social mobility through occupation, education, or private economic entrepreneurship is relatively limited. For all of them these initial gains proved to be an unbeatable combination of permanent advantages over their opponents.

THE EXTENSION OF POLITICAL PARTICIPATION

Within a few years, mostly as a result of the pressures exerted by African nationalists, the electorate was enlarged until practically all adults were eligible to vote. At the same time the authority of representative councils and of African executives was widened until, immediately before independence, it extended over most aspects of public life expect for foreign affairs, defense, and related matters. Politics became more complex. In order to be successful, organizations had to mobilize support from much larger bodies of people and compete with an increasing number of political entrepreneurs drawn into the game once the risks of punishment had practically disappeared and the rewards had become more tangible.

From the point of view of the initial mass movements, what occurred can be summarized as two contrary trends: on the one hand, the mass movements benefited from a bandwagon effect; on the other, they faced the threat of fragmentation. The paradox is superficial only; both processes stem from the character of the masses which were being mobilized politically during this period.

The bandwagon effect as used here is borrowed from the literature on American political behavior. It was formulated as an attempt to reconcile the widely held belief, verified by repeated surveys, that nonvoters tended to favor the Democratic party (a generalization which made sense since both partisan outlook and voting turnout were known to be related to social class) with the surprising finding that the post-election surveys of 1952 and 1956 dealt this notion a severe blow; by the latter year, only about one-quarter of the non-voters indicating a preference said they would have voted Democratic. The authors of *The American Voter* reasoned as follows: the non-voter is less involved in politics; hence he can be expected to be less stable in his partisan inclinations than the voter "and more responsive to the massive political stimuli that produce shifts of popular attitude over time;" hence, they concluded, "We have little doubt that for the non-voter a stimulus of great importance in this period, as in any other, was the fact of who was winning elections. For at least part of the way between his position of 1948 and his position of 1956 the non-voter was riding a psychological bandwagon."[24]

To apply this notion uncritically to so widely different a population as that of West African countries would be reckless. Nevertheless, the basic notion that uninvolved individuals respond to the most powerful available stimulus, such as the one provided by a leading personality or an apparently powerful organization, is perhaps relatively independent of the cultural context. The sort of research that would be needed to verify this hypothesis was unfortunately not carried out in West Africa when it was feasible. Nevertheless, there are a few meager clues which suggest that a similar phenomenon did occur and indeed contributed heavily to the later success of the mass movement and perhaps even to the general trend toward the emergence of a single party. Birmingham and Jahoda, who conducted a survey of participation at the time of the 1954 elections in Ghana, suggest that in Accra, affiliation of individuals to parties and candidates *opposed* to the CPP tended to be mediated by personal links. But in the *absence* of such links, "voters seemed to fall in with the powerful propaganda of the CPP."[25]

Another observer of the Ghanaian scene confirms this phenomenon and suggests that it is fully compatible with traditional political culture. Discussing Ashanti, Austin writes:

> The fact that the NLM was in the ascendant in 1956, and the CPP on the defensive, helped to tilt the balance still farther on the side of the Ashanti party. The overall victory of the CPP in the

---

[24]A. Campbell, P. Converse, W. Miller, and D. Stokes, *The American Voter* (New York: John Wiley & Sons, 1960), p. 111.

[25]Walter Birmingham and Gustav Jahoda, "A Pre-Election Survey in a Semi-Literate Society," *Public Opinion Quarterly* (Summer, 1955), p. 152.

election then saw the balance tilt back in favour of the ruling party. All power attracts and—in Ghana—the exercise of absolute power tended to attract absolutely. Or, in more homely terms: "Obi nmi sono akyi mmoro huasu"—If one follows the elephant, the dew from the leaves does not wet one's clothes.[26]

The tendency toward one-party dominant regions in Nigeria has been accounted for in similar terms[27]; and while I cannot cite evidence from personal observation to confirm the existence of this phenomenon, it is fully compatible with my own general understanding of the political process in the countries with which I am most familiar. In other words, as participation was extended, a large number of people hitherto uninvolved in politics identified with the dominant party unless there was a strong reason—usually involving primary group ties—for not doing so.

This hypothesis is also compatible with the opposite effect to which we now turn, fragmentation. In the Ivory Coast and in Ghana, and to a lesser extent in Senegal, after the initial success of the mass movement a number of other political organizations arose to challenge its supremacy. Although some of these parties benefited from the support of the colonial authorities, this cannot account for the persistence of the phenomenon nor for its near-universality. Furthermore, in almost every election, there was almost as much danger from splintering as there was from outside challenges. Once the principle of African participation in government had been established and the road to self-government cleared, competition for control of the new institutions was intensified as new political entrepreneurs entered into the game. At the same time, many individuals relatively uninvolved until that time, such as traditional leaders or men who had been reluctant earlier to engage in popular politics, believed that they might have a greater stake in the outcome; within the movement itself, many leaders below the top who were most familiar with the game thought they might take a chance on becoming the top leaders of other movements. What sorts of social differentiation were available in these societies to form new bases of political support? What strong reason could be elicited from the masses for not identifying with the dominant movement?

---

[26]Austin, p. 315.
[27]For example, James S. Coleman commented on this for Nigeria in C. Grove Haines, *Africa Today* (Baltimore: Johns Hopkins Press, 1956), p. 239n. See also J. Mackintosh, "Electoral Trends and the Tendency to a One-Party System in Nigeria," *Journal of Commonwealth Political Studies,* I, No. 3 (November, 1962), 194–210.

For the most part it entailed an appeal to primordial loyalties, usually in the form of ethnic affinities—using this term broadly to include subgroups within a larger one—or kinship relationships. This tendency was reinforced by the fact that as political participation was extended, the new electorate included more of the rural population, composed much less of transitionals than of traditionals, who would naturally be more responsive to appropriate stimuli. As the political sphere was enlarged, there was a general politicization of primordial ties.[28]

Most important, from the point of view of the dominant mass movement, this process often involved splintering within its own midst; as political entrepreneurs chipped away at the loose coalition it represented, there was a danger that the nationalist movement itself might be turned into nothing but another ethnic or regional organization through the loss of all but the most solid core of its supporters. Once this process began, the bandwagon effect could also work *against* the initially dominant movement, as already illustrated above by Austin. The same characteristics that had facilitated the early mobilization of the masses by the nationalist movement also were the source of its greatest weakness: in mass politics, loyalties do not go very deep, apathy can easily return after the initial spurt of enthusiasm, and the masses can then become reactivated by a new set of leaders. How these conflicting trends affected the dominant movements can be seen in a brief consideration of their organization and electoral performance during this later period.

The case of Ghana is particularly valuable because there were more observers there and hence more information was gathered at the time. The CPP was reorganized in 1952 "in order to exercise a closer control from headquarters."[29] In his study of Gold Coast politics shortly afterwards, Apter viewed the party as "the most effective mass political organization in Africa" and reported that "in its largest sense, the party can be dubbed a Tammany-type machine with a nationalist ideology. In a more specific sense, it is composed of a militant elect who dominate and spearhead the nationalist movement, having their own highly disciplined nucleus."[30] Organizationally, Apter states, the CPP was a composite of the British Labour party and a Communist

---

[28] For these concepts, see Clifford Geertz, "The Integrative Revolution," in Clifford Geertz (ed.), *Old Societies and New States* (New York: The Free Press of Glencoe, 1963), pp. 105-57.
[29] Austin, p. 171.
[30] David Apter, *The Gold Coast in Transition* (Princeton: Princeton University Press, 1955), p. 202.

party. A French observer a little later reached the conclusion that the CPP's organization "is more revolutionary even than its program."[31] Bretton, who visited Ghana in 1956, stated that it would be appropriate, "but without reference to ideological orientation, to compare the CPP with Communist or Fascist parties, making allowance for organizational deficiencies."[32] Are these the blind men trying to identify what we know to be an elephant? What sort of hybrid creature was the CPP? Austin reconciles these various views by concluding that "if the analogy were not faintly ridiculous in so warm-blooded a country, one might say that between 1951 and 1954 the CPP showed, as does an iceberg, only its surface structure to the casual observer."[33] His own account confirms Apter's reference to a Tammany-type machine, and hence all but destroys the relevance of Communist and Fascist organizational models. There were indeed national executive bodies and many liaison committees, but on the whole the national leaders had little control over the movement, which had come to reflect the heterogeneity of local interests and pressures. Discipline may have impressed some observers, but certainly not Kwame Nkrumah, who complained bitterly of its absence in his own autobiography.[34]

We can go one step beyond such general descriptions and try to estimate the hold the CPP had achieved over the Gold Coast on the eve of independence. The adult population was estimated at about 2.4 million, and estimates of membership made during the period 1952–56 vary from 400,000 to 1,200,000 (the latter including "sympathizers") with widely divergent figures for any given year. How useful these figures are is debatable since Austin warns that dues were often not paid or that when they were paid at the local level they seldom reached Accra headquarters.[35] Austin speaks of 500 branches by the end of 1952, Apter of 2,885 local offices in 1953, and Boyon again of

---

[31] J. Boyon, *Naissance d'un Etat Africain: Le Ghana* (Paris: Librairie Armand Colin, 1958), p. 161.

[32] Henry L. Bretton, "Current Political Thought and Practice in Ghana," *The American Political Science Review*, LII (March, 1958), 57.

[33] Austin, p. 175.

[34] Kwame Nkrumah, *Ghana: The Autobiography of Kwame Nkrumah* (Edinburgh: Thomas Nelson & Sons, 1959), p. 209.

[35] Details of these estimates are as follows: Austin reports 700,000 for the latter part of 1952 (Austin, pp. 171–76); Apter, warning that caution must be used, reports a claim of over a million members for 1953 (p. 217); Richard Wright, in *Black Power, A Record of Reactions in a Land of Pathos* (New York: Harper and Brothers, 1954), p. 106, estimated 400,000 the same year "mainly of the petty bourgeois class"; Boyon refers to 700,000 active registered members and 500,000 sympathizers around 1955–56 (p. 161).

3,000 sections in 1955–56[36] As a check on these figures, we may refer to electoral support obtained by the CPP under a system of near-universal adult suffrage:

ELECTORAL SUPPORT FOR THE CPP

	1954	1956
Total CPP Votes	391,817	398,141
Per Cent of Total Votes Cast	55	57
Per Cent of Registered Voters	32	28.5
Per Cent of Estimated Adult Population	16	15

From these we may conclude that although nearly 6 out of 10 adults who voted in a given election cast their lot with the CPP—which thus did a little better than its opponents could do—the party, after many years of effort and in spite of all the advantages discussed, could mobilize, to the extent of having them register and vote, only about one out of six or seven adult Ghanaians. Furthermore, the party's strength varied widely from area to area. Of the total number of local party offices reported by Apter for around 1953, three-quarters were in the Colony and in Ashanti; the party's organization was much weaker in Trans-Volta–Togoland and almost skeletal in the North, a fact confirmed by Austin. Similarly, the electoral strength of the CPP was much more evident in the southern areas in 1954 and weaker in the Northern Territories; by 1956, the distribution had shifted somewhat, but a strong skewing of distribution was still clearly visible:

REGIONAL DISTRIBUTION OF CPP STRENGTH[37]
(CPP votes as per cent of total votes cast)

	1954	1956
Colony	67	84
Ashanti	58	43
Trans-Volta–Togoland	54	55
Northern Territories	37	43

Although the charge made by the CPP's opponents that by 1956 it had become a mere southern regional party was not true—after all, more than half of the total votes it received came from *outside* the Colony area—it was clear that the bandwagon effect persisted in the region of its birth and most intensive activity, while the process of fragmentation

---

[36] Austin, p. 171; Apter, p. 217; Boyon, p. 161.
[37] Based on figures from Austin, pp. 244, 354.

was clearly visible elsewhere. Although the party's electoral victories were decisive—it obtained 72 out of 104 seats in the 1956 elections—the ease with which determined opponents, such as the leaders of the NLM in Ashanti, could subvert large blocks of supporters from the movement revealed the fundamentally fragile nature of its hold over the part of the population it controlled at the time.

Because of important differences in circumstances and timing, the case of the Ivory Coast is not exactly parallel to that of Ghana. Nevertheless, there are close similarities if we take into account the period from 1948 to 1951. By then the PDCI had also been able to mobilize support, and its symbols as well as the names of its leaders had become bywords in many parts of the country. This enabled the party to persist even when other groups, supported by the French administration, arose in the major cultural regions of the country, much as they did in Ghana later on. Afterwards the party became a political machine, even though it did not control the territorial executive, through the activities of its leaders in Paris. Locally, the formal organization of the party, with its network of branches and committees, was even farther from its paper model than it had been earlier, as indicated by the decline in the payment of party dues. Nevertheless, it served admirably as an electoral organization, and a French observer who witnessed the 1956 elections said of it that "one is almost tempted to call it a native para-government."[38]

The 1957 elections in French-speaking West Africa were comparable to the 1956 election in Ghana in that they were also the first to be based on universal suffrage. The PDCI candidates obtained 89 per cent of the votes cast and all but 2 of the 60 seats in the Territorial Assembly. With a turnout of 54 per cent of those registered, this represented about 49 per cent of the potential electorate. Did these figures mean that the PDCI had been more successful than the CPP in mobilizing the population? This question is difficult to answer. Different registration procedures which insured that almost all individuals qualified to vote would be included tended, given the bandwagon effect, to benefit the majority party.[39] An additional advantage to large parties stemmed from the division of the country into much larger constituencies than those in Ghana: a total of 19 to Ghana's 104, with

---

[38] M. Vignaud, "Les élections du 2 janvier 1956 en Côte d'Ivoire," *Revue Française de Science Politique,* VI, No. 3 (July–September, 1956), 570–82.

[39] For registration procedures and their effects, see Kenneth Robinson, "Senegal: The Elections of the Territorial Assembly, March, 1957," in W. J. M. Mackenzie and K. E. Robinson (eds.), *Five Elections in Africa* (Oxford: Clarendon Press, 1960), p. 346; and Austin, pp. 109–10.

only about half the latter's population. Territorial solidarity, enhanced at this time because of the stand the country had taken on important issues concerning the Federation of French West Africa, may have affected the turnout. The generally weaker position of traditional authorities in French-speaking Africa deprived the Ivory Coast ethnic parties of the sort of ready-made organization through chiefs and their councils available to its counterparts in Ghana. The ethnic groups were smaller and more numerous; the nearest equivalent to the Ashanti people are the Baoule, but their loyalty to the PDCI was relatively secure since it is the tribe to which Houphouet-Boigny himself belongs. Nevertheless, the process of fragmentation was still visible albeit in a more latent form, as demonstrated by the fact that most of the districts in which opposition candidates had secured substantial support in 1951 still ran opposition candidates in 1957.[40]

As the oldest French colony in Africa, Senegal has a longer tradition than most African countries of territorial identity; in addition, the existence of a *lingua franca* and the nearly universal penetration of Islam have facilitated the growth of a sense of nationality.[41] One would therefore expect the process of ethnic fragmentation to be less threatening to the dominant movement; yet even here "such [ethnic] feeling, long concealed by the iron grid of the French administration in pre-war years, now emerged."[42] As political participation was extended following the initial victory of Senghor's organization in 1951, the Lebou of the Dakar area, the people of the Casamance region, and the Fulani acted as relatively autonomous political blocs, moving in and out of the party. In spite of the attempt in 1954 to transform an indirect party, a coalition of "clans" and ethnic groups, into a more direct one, Robinson reported that the differentiations between the original components were not abolished but rather transferred from without to within the party, where they remained to plague the leadership.[43]

By 1957, the *Bloc Populaire Sénégalais* (BPS) claimed from 165,000 to 180,000 members, but it was difficult to determine whether these were genuine activists or whether the branches had acquired a large number of party cards at the last minute in order to increase their representation at the party congress. The party had decided to create many new branches, but "it was frankly admitted at the party congress that not

---

[40] See *One-Party Government in the Ivory Coast*, pp. 200–201.
[41] M. Crowder, *Senegal: A Study in French Assimilation Policy* (London: Oxford University Press, 1962), p. 84.
[42] Robinson, "Senegal: The Elections . . .," p. 320.
[43] *Ibid.*, pp. 320, 337.

even a beginning had been made in establishing them." As for the existing ones, "in many rural areas they had a somewhat formal existence." On the whole, Robinson concludes that the BPS put more emphasis on organization than its major rival, the Socialists; although the distribution and character of branches for both parties was about even, "it would be fair to say that the BPS network was much more nearly universal."[44]

In the light of the BPS's continued success, Robinson's cautious appraisal confirms the central theme of this chapter, namely, that it is more reasonable to attribute the success of dominant parties to marginal increments of organization and to the cumulative consequences of the political process in West Africa than to any overwhelming historical force or to an overwhelmingly superior organizational structure. In spite of its unimpressive character, the BPS obtained 78 per cent of the votes cast in 1957—about 41 per cent of the registered vote, with 80 to 95 per cent majorities along the coast and in the Sine-Saloum peanut-growing areas which constitute a sort of Wolof-Serere ethnic core region. Within this core, the Lingere area dissented, perhaps because of long-standing historical antagonism between this historic seat of the Djoloff state and the remainder of the region.[45] The BPS was also weaker in the Futa Toro region, the original area of Tukulor expansion from which attempts to dominate Wolof and Serere states had been launched in the past; in a district dominated by the Malinke, who have greater cultural affinities with dominant groups in Guinea and Mali than with the rest of Senegal; and in Dakar and Saint-Louis where the Socialists held on to a dominant position buttressed by several decades of political tradition. Here, as in Ghana and in the Ivory Coast, it is difficult to tell whether the bandwagon effect in the long run would have offset the tendency toward fragmentation since the natural interplay of these processes was drastically interrupted once the leaders of the dominant party obtained full control over the rules of the political game.

BELATED TRIUMPHS

Before concluding this chapter we shall examine the cases of Guinea and Sudan (now Mali), which present an interesting contrast

---

[44]*Ibid.*, pp. 339–42.
[45]The historical background can be found in J. S. Trimingham, *A History of Islam in West Africa* (London: Oxford University Press, 1962), pp. 172ff.

with the three other countries because in Guinea and Sudan the mass movement triumphed much later after occupying a minority position for nearly a decade after its founding. That "patron" parties were able to hold the center of the stage for so long can be attributed in part to the assistance and support they received from the French administration. If that were a sufficient explanation, however, it would seem to indicate that mass movements could not have triumphed unless they had benefited from the complex of circumstances discussed earlier. This proposition exaggerates the degree to which the colonial administration could act without regard for political realities. In reality, when the mass movement survived in spite of all, partly because of tangible assistance from equivalent movements in other parts of French West Africa, the French decided, albeit reluctantly, to consider them as the *interlocuteur valable* in Mali and Guinea as well. Then the marginal increment of organization came fully into play and insured the victory of the *Parti Démocratique de Guinée* (PDG) and of the *Union Soudanaise* (US) of Mali.

The leading political organization in Guinea after the war was the Socialist party; it was built around the administrative machinery of the *chefs de canton* with the support of the French and drew support primarily from the Fulani of the Futa-Djalon region.[46] Here too, as elsewhere in French West Africa, the nucleus of a territorial section of the RDA was launched as well. Founded by a Sudanese (Malian), Madeira Keita, it had as one of its major components the postal workers' union founded and led by Sékou Touré. Both men were associated with the *Groupe d'Etudes Communistes* and benefited from the technical assistance it provided; both were Malinke; Keita bore the name of the founders of the ancient kingdom of Mali, while Touré was a descendant of Almamy Samory Touré, a Muslim warrior of the nineteenth century renowned for his resistance to European penetration.

Because of the existence of a Socialist machine, their organization, known from 1947 on as the PDG, did not have the advantage of its Ivory Coast counterpart in moving into a vacuum and securing widespread support before the French administration launched an all-out offensive against the RDA everywhere. The PDG almost disappeared between 1948 and 1951, except in the trade-union milieu of Conakry

---

[46]Sékou Touré's own account of political beginnings is in *Expérience Guinéenne et Unité Africaine* (Paris: Présence Africaine, 1962), p. 11. See also Ruth Morgenthau, *Political Parties* . . ., Ch. VI.

and in N'Zerekore, a Malinke border district, where it was sustained by the support of Ivoirien activists who organized farmers' strikes against the forced delivery of agricultural products.[47] The French played an active role in determining electoral results until 1953–54. In 1951, no party could be called truly dominant. The leading Socialists had only 30.4 per cent of the votes, and had to share even the Fulani areas with other regional competitors.[48] The PDG obtained only 14 per cent, mainly in N'Zerekore, Malinke areas, and Conakry. Sékou Touré reorganized the party in 1952 and became its secretary-general, but was defeated in a local election that year. The following year, however, he won a seat in the Territorial Assembly, allegedly after the Governor-General of French West Africa, probably under pressure from RDA leaders elsewhere, personally intervened to insure fair play in the by-elections.[49]

It was during the next three years that the PDG truly became a nationalist movement, following a spurt of organizational expansion comparable to that of the CPP in 1949–51 and the PDCI in 1947–49. The launching of a series of major industrial projects (mining and hydroelectric plants) from 1952 on suddenly created an industrial labor force which Sékou Touré rapidly transformed into a militant trade-union movement. Before 1953, union membership was about 2,600; by 1955, after a successful strike brought Sékou Touré into the limelight, it had risen to 39,000.[50] Left headless by the death of its leader in 1954, the Socialist party was further weakened by the struggle for succession. With the help of an RDA all-star team from other territories and additional funds provided by the RDA the PDG improved its position considerably in the territory-wide by-election held that year. It remained strong in Conakry; in the new industrial areas support grew from 1–5 per cent in 1951 to over 75 per cent in 1954; and the party continued to spread into the Malinke areas. The Fulani districts, except on the periphery (where there was a mixed popula-

---

[47]Bernard Charles, "Un parti politique africain: le Parti Démocratique de Guinée," *Revue Française de Science Politique*, XII, No. 2 (June, 1962), 313. See also L. Gray Cowan, "Guinea," in Gwendolen M. Carter (ed.), *African One-Party States* (Ithaca: Cornell University Press, 1961), pp. 149–86.

[48]The electoral data and much of the analysis are based on J. Beaujeu-Garnier, "Essai de géographie électorale Guinéenne," *Cahiers d'Outre-Mer*, No. 4 (1958), 309–38.

[49]Ernest Milcent, *L'AOF entre en scène*," (Paris: La Bibliothèque de l'Homme d'Action, 1958), p. 89n.

[50]See Franz Ansprenger, *Politik im Schwarzen Africa* (Köln: Westdeutscher Verlag, 1961), pp. 142–43.

tion) and in Mamou, where the PDG benefited from the support of a particular Fulani family, voted almost unanimously for the *Bloc Africain de Guinée* (BAG), an ethnic coalition which obtained a total of 63 per cent of the votes. But this apparent Fulani homogeneity masked an important sociological fact: about one-third of the population of these areas consisted of serf-like "captives" who, when political participation was enlarged, responded en masse to the promise of freedom held out by the PDG.[51]

To his prominence as the descendant of Samory and as the hero of the 1953 strike, Sékou Touré added recognition by the Europeans as a "governor" in 1955, under the circumstances mentioned earlier. The same year, Saifoulaye Diallo, his Fulani ally, returned from Upper Volta; in 1956 he shared the PDG ticket with Sékou Touré and thus brought several new areas into the party. Progress was spectacular: with a 105 per cent increase in eligible voters since 1954, the PDG increased its own votes by 288 per cent while the BAG actually went down from 140,000 to 132,000, as if it had reached the limit of its capacity to enlist support. Minor parties were reduced to sharing 12 per cent of the total. The following year Sékou Touré, by then *député* in the French National Assembly and mayor of the capital city, led his party to the final triumph: with 81 per cent of the votes, the PDG obtained all but 4 seats in the Territorial Assembly. The movement had thus been able to mobilize about 40 per cent of the adult population, at least to the extent of bringing them to the polls, while its opponents were limited to only about 14 per cent, mostly from a particular region. Equally important, however, was the fact that nearly half of the population of Guinea had not yet been activated by the time the PDG became the government.

Of the groups that arose in the French Sudan after the war, three were of particular interest. One was a trade-union organization affiliated with the *Groupe d'Etudes Communistes* (GEC) in the same manner as the PDG nucleus in Guinea. Two others were led by schoolteachers, Mamadou Konaté and Fily Dabo Sissoko, both of whom were members of the same generation, came from the same part of the country, and were highly respected by European officials. Although all three groups were temporarily unified when the RDA held its founding congress in Bamako in October, 1946, they soon split up into two separate organizations. Fily Dabo Sissoko formed the *Parti Souda-*

---

[51] Pierre et Renée Gosset, *L'Afrique, les Africains* (Paris: Julliard, 1958), I, 82.

nais Progressiste (PSP), based like the Socialist party in Guinea on the *chef de canton* network, with particular support from the Fulani and the Sarakolle, who together constitute about one-fourth of the total population, and from the traditional trading bourgeoisies of the ancient cities of the Western Sudan.[52] Mamadou Konaté, with some younger men such as the Malinke teacher Modibo Keita and the Bambara leader of the trade-union group, Idrissa Diarra, formed the *Union Soudanaise* (US), territorial section of the RDA. The US drew much support from the Malinke areas, from which many of its founders came and where the Keita name insured respect; from the Sikasso area, where Modibo Keita had been stationed as a teacher; from the city of Bamako, and towns and villages along the railroad line, where unions were most active; and from lower caste groups and "captives," much as did the PDG. Its leaders did not neglect the other end of the social scale, however, and the party's fortunes in the highly traditional *Boucle du Niger* region rose rapidly when it obtained the support of the ruling Haidara family of Timbuktu and the Maigas and Tourés in Gao. In spite of the radical tone of its ideology, the US seemed to be intent on creating a coalition between the descendants of two ancient empires—Mali and Songhai—which had in turn dominated much of the area of contemporary Sudan.

Political participation extended slowly in the Sudan, a much less developed country than the others we have considered. Although nearly half the adult population was qualified to vote in 1952, only about 29 per cent of those eligible actually went to the polls.[53] The US's share, which had been about one-third of the votes in 1946 and 1951, rose to 40 per cent. Here as in Guinea, the big organizational spurt occurred between 1952 and 1956. These efforts, together with the benefits derived from the general rise of the RDA in French West Africa and the removal of administrative pressure, enabled the US to move in where the PSP had not yet penetrated, gaining the support of a variety of groups and at the same time losing less support from the constant fragmentation which plagued all parties. In the January, 1956, elections, although the size of the registered electorate and the regional distribution of strength between the two contenders remained about the same as they had been, the PSP was able to secure only 30

---

[52] For the early years, see in particular, J. Delval, "Le RDA au Soudan Français," *L'Afrique et l'Asie*, No. 16 (1951), 54–67.

[53] These electoral data are drawn from my own unpublished notes.

per cent more votes than in 1952, while the US doubled its total. For the first time it became the leading party, with a little under half of the votes cast, while the PSP obtained only 37 per cent, and the remainder was scattered among smaller groups including splinters from both PSP and US. The death of Mamadou Konaté, founder of the US and successful arbiter of its internal conflicts, shortly after this election might have been disastrous if the party had not benefited during the ensuing by-election from the presence of a high-powered RDA team which included such well-known men as Ouezzin Coulibaly and Sékou Touré. Voter turnout dropped to 25 per cent, but although the US gained fewer votes than in January, the PSP suffered an even greater loss and the US emerged with 60 per cent of the total.

Clearly, these results would not have been obtained had the US not been more efficient than its opponents. But what did this entail in absolute terms? Ruth Morgenthau, who was doing field work in the region at about this time, has written that the US managed to hold its heterogeneous components together "because it was remarkably well organized"; although the party formally resembled other RDA sections, it was "special in its operations," led by men who had much interest in theory, gave great attention to detail, kept records, and maintained a good network of communications.[54] This characterization is somewhat more impressive than the candid self-portrait of the organization which was revealed at the fifth congress held in 1958.[55] The total paid-up membership, represented by 215 voting delegates, was between 50,000 and 60,000. They were organized into 56 *sous-sections* or committees, one-fifth of them constituted by the wards of Bamako, the capital city. The others were located in administrative centers throughout the country, but their organization seldom reached below them to the village level. Many of the delegates sent to the congress by the branches were residents of Bamako rather than field workers, and the branches very irregularly sent reports of their activities to the ruling organs. These delegates elected the *bureau politique,* territorial executive, at congresses held annually in theory, but every three years in practice. This body, together with one delegate per *cercle,* again generally residents of Bamako (a total of 18),

---

[54]Morgenthau, *Political Parties,* p. 291.
[55]Union Soudanaise, RDA, "Documents," (Bamako, 1959; mimeographed) and *L'Essor,* special issue, August 16, 1958. Membership figures were not published but it was stated at the congress that each of the 215 delegates represented between 250 and 300 members.

and 11 representatives of the Bamako *cercle* constituted the *Comité Directeur,* which acted as a sort of party parliament occasionally convened between congresses. In addition, the US had a loosely affiliated ancillary youth organization and some women's committees. It published a daily newspaper, then in its ninth year, which had recently grown from one to two mimeographed pages, and from a daily circulation of 300 to 500. As late as 1959, when I first visited the country, the party had its headquarters in a rented Bamako shop usually manned by the political secretary and one or two typists, along with a French Communist factotum inherited from the early days.

This, then, was the US, a year after it had gained control of the executive in the territory. With this organization it was able in 1957 to obtain 68 per cent of the votes cast and all but 6 seats in the Territorial Assembly. Altogether, during the five-year period beginning in 1952, during which the registered electorate nearly doubled, the PSP had been able to gain only 50 per cent over its 1952 base, while the US increased its support fourfold. Yet electoral participation remained low and hence the total number of votes for the US constituted but one-fifth of the estimated adult population of the country.

CONCLUSIONS

Besides supplying a general historical background, we have attempted in this chapter to stress two major themes. The first concerns the characteristics of the nationalist movement and their implications for our understanding of the political process in West Africa. That an organization can bring even one-fifth of the population to the polls in a country as undeveloped as Mali, for example, where physical communications are extremely poor, where literacy is low even by African standards, and where in general there has been little exposure to modernity, is a truly remarkable achievement. Its indication of the political acumen and the determination of the leadership is highlighted by the fact that all their opponents combined never managed to do better than half as well. Relatively speaking, therefore, the nationalist movements constituted a superior form of organization. But it would be misleading to view even the most effective of them as an organizational juggernaut. The working data we have were gathered by a handful of keen observers, but it mattered a great deal *when* they saw the party in operation, whether before an election or a congress, or during some less exciting period; and it is difficult to sift out reliable personal observations from information gathered from a few officials and party documents. Robinson, writing about Senegal in 1957, expressed the problem well:

> It is thus extremely difficult to characterize the nature of the party organizations at the onset of the elections. It is always difficult to move from discussing the formal constitution of a political party to a realistic account of how it works; this difficulty is increased in countries (like those of Africa) in which the formal constitution of the party is derived from foreign models and is silent about vital factors in party formation and activity which are on the contrary derived from the social and cultural environment of Africa. But in this case there is the further difficulty that party organization was in a particularly fluid state and the relation between formal constitution and the realities of party organization was all the more uncertain.[56]

An additional problem stems from what might be called the developmental phase of the movement at the time it was observed. Clearly, parties everywhere were more exciting, more enthusiastic, more bustling with activity during what we called the initial organizational spurt. This occurred in the Ivory Coast around 1947–49, in Senegal in 1948–51, in Ghana in 1949–51, but in Guinea and in Mali quite a bit later, around 1954–56. After this original spurt the party tended to slow down to daily business. In 1956, for example, the PDCI or the BPS appeared less impressive organizationally than the PDG or the US; Apter's impressions of the CPP when he revisited Ghana around the time of independence were different from what they had been four years earlier.[57] This not only affected observers and hence the generalizations made about the parties, but also the very shape of the state. It helps to explain why the two latecomers, the PDG and the US, gave birth to regimes which appeared much more mobilizing or "revolutionary" than any of the others.

But it is difficult to believe, on the basis of the evidence available, that under existing circumstances the capacity of these movements for "mobilization" extended much beyond intermittent electioneering and the collection of more tangible support in the form of party dues from

---

[56]Robinson, "Senegal: The Elections . . .," p. 335.
[57]David Apter, "What's Happening in Ghana?" *Africa Special Report,* November, 1957, pp. 1, 2, 12–13.

a tiny fraction of the population. Although their ambition was often to extend tentacles throughout society, they were creatures with a relatively large head in the capital and fairly rudimentary limbs. They spoke the language of democratic centralism, with stress on both the democratic and the disciplinary implications of the concept, but internal structures of communication, accountability, and control operated only intermittently. Thus, although the distinction between "mass" and "cadre" and "patron" party is suggestive and useful, it must not be overly reified, lest we erect an analytic model on a tenuous empirical foundation. It is also an oversimplification to view the process as one of "mass" parties superseding "cadre" parties in a sort of vulgar Darwinism.

The second theme pertains to the tendency toward the emergence of single-party systems. In each case considered here, one political organization had emerged which held the center of the stage and could more appropriately be called a nationalist movement than any of its opponents. These movements were not necessarily devoid of ethnic and other traditional particularisms; on the contrary, most of them grew by successfully incorporating a variety of ethnic and other groups. The difference was that these coalitions were large, and hence by definition had to be heterogeneous, while many of their opponents almost by default stressed specific affiliations. The extent to which these parties were truly dominant varied; if electoral performance is used—and it is the most reliable criterion available—then the parties of Senegal, Ivory Coast, and Guinea were clearly different from those of Mali and Ghana, where it looked, toward the end of this period, as if something more like a two-party system was being institutionalized. Given the tendencies we have noted, it is likely that the natural outcome would not have been a one-party state, but rather a pattern similar to that in India, where the nationalist movement has continued to undergo a process of splintering and of amalgamation, remaining dominant and different from all other organizations, but never achieving a monopoly of access to political office at all levels.

That the outcome was different stems from the fundamental fact that the rules of the political game were drastically altered when the nationalist movement achieved control over them—after independence in Ghana, even before independence in some of the French-speaking countries. To understand how the single-party state emerged in the form we know, it is not sufficient to investigate sociological or cultural tendencies. It was a goal set by a political elite which then worked self-consciously for its achievement. How this particular goal was selected and the manner in which it was pursued will be considered in the chapters that follow. It will be important to remember that the latent tendencies of the societies in which these political processes occur militate *against* the one-party state. Hence, it is to be expected that there will be a constant tension between the regime and the society.

CHAPTER II

THE ONE-PARTY IDEOLOGY

RESPONSES TO STRAIN

IT IS DIFFICULT TO DETERMINE PRECISELY WHEN THE TRANSFORMATION OF political systems in which one party was dominant into a new type which we shall call the West African party-state began, in part because there were many continuities. Although in reality Africans formulated theories and modified processes and institutions concurrently, we shall consider these aspects separately in this and the following chapters.

The idea of a dominant party was already common during the nationalist phase. As Hodgkin has indicated in his excellent analysis of the language of African nationalism, one of its tenets was that the people in colonial territories constituted a nation in the process of becoming; hence a national liberation movement with a broad base was needed to set things right; in such a movement, elites acted in the name of the masses with a double legitimacy as successors to precolonial states and as spokesmen for the general will.[1] In French-speaking Africa the achievement of political unity was sought first at the interterritorial level and then at the territorial level from 1946 on. Although it was not achieved for French West Africa as a whole, and it was achieved for the territories only *after* self-government, the norm of the single, all-encompassing movement was never abandoned. A leader of the RDA stated in 1957, for example, "No underdeveloped country which reached its political maturity was able to do so without giving primacy to a single political party, or to one with such an over-

---

[1] Thomas Hodgkin, "A Note on the Language of African Nationalism," reprinted in William John Hanna (ed.), *Independent Black Africa* (Chicago: Rand McNally, 1964), pp. 235–52.

whelming majority that it controlled every sector of social life."[2] Whether or not this is historically correct, what matters is that men believed that it was.

This idea was reinforced by the practical requirements engendered by the process of decolonization: it owed much to the bargaining atmosphere which prevailed, when the right of the dominant parties to act in the name of the whole people of a territory was under constant scrutiny. In Ghana, for example, the growth of dissent in Ashanti after 1954 prompted a reconsideration of the schedule of independence. Although the CPP maintained a solid majority in Parliament, the British did not deem this sufficient:

> The Secretary of State estimated that the British Government would hesitate to grant independence to the Gold Coast until a substantial majority of the people had shown that they wanted independence in the very near future and had agreed upon a workable constitution for the country.[3]

Similarly, although the PDCI obtained 89 per cent of the votes cast and all but two seats in the Territorial Assembly in 1957, some French commentators stressed the fact that only 54 per cent of the population had participated and hinted that this indicated the existence of a silent opposition to Houphouet-Boigny's policies, a reasoning which would apply to most American Presidential elections during this century, when participation has ranged between 50 and 60 per cent.[4] Whether or not such an inference was warranted, Ivoirien leaders acknowledged that the results were unsatisfactory. The following year, partly because of the Gaullist plebiscitary mood, it was mandatory for the Ivory Coast to demonstrate overwhelming support for a "yes" just as it was mandatory in Guinea to demonstrate unanimity for "no" on the issue of adherence to the French Community. Participation was above 85 per cent in both cases and majorities above 95 per cent.

Thus, in most of West Africa, a sort of political inflation set in at about the time of independence. Once such a precedent as that of the

---

[2] Quoted in André Blanchet, *L'Itinéraire des Partis Africains depuis Bamako* (Paris: Plon, 1958), p. 202.

[3] Kwame Nkrumah, *Ghana: The Autobiography of Kwame Nkrumah* (Edinburgh: Thomas Nelson & Sons, 1959), p. 202.

[4] See the author's *One-Party Government in the Ivory Coast* (Princeton: Princeton University Press, 1964), p. 215.

1958 referendum was set, it was difficult to depart from it; equally large majorities could be construed as a catastrophic loss of support when accompanied by lower participation. Once some countries did it, others had to follow suit lest their regimes be viewed as less popular than their neighbor's.

Increasingly, however, beneath the jubilation that accompanied the achievement of self-government and independence in most of West Africa, the new rulers seemed to fall prey to a much less sanguine mood, as if after having labored for years to reach the political summit they suddenly looked down for the first time and were dizzied by the immense uncharted vistas that appeared before them. The assumption of responsibility for the affairs of the new states produced a shocking awareness of the magnitude of the burdens of government in an underdeveloped country. At one level, this crisis can be viewed as a source of great psychological pressure on individuals. As Leonard Doob has suggested, modern Africans are caught up between two cultures, their own traditional one and that of modern Europe, and must grope for their own way. "This discrepancy between what is on the one hand and what was or what could be on the other hand must continue to persist during a period of rapid change."[5] They believe, according to Doob, that the European way is superior to the African, but are forced defensively to assert confidence in themselves. When power is transferred from a European to an African elite, "Most Africans must feel, consequently, that only the source but not the fact of their impotence has changed."[6] Although most people are not affected by this crisis, those who are fully involved in the process because of the roles they occupy "seem significantly uncertain."[7]

These strains are not merely psychological or sociological, but cultural as well, stemming, so to speak, from a sudden confrontation with an unknown region with inadequate maps.[8] Not only are the new rulers new at their jobs, but in a fundamental sense their jobs are new as well because of the very different conceptions of government that prevail in a colonial dependency and in a new nation. During the

---

[5] Leonard Doob, "The Psychological Pressures upon Modern Africans," *Journal of Human Relations*, VIII, Nos. 3 and 4 (Spring–Summer 1960), 467.
[6] *Ibid.*, p. 468.
[7] *Ibid.*, p. 470.
[8] I owe this thought and much of the approach used in this chapter to my colleague Clifford Geertz, and in particular to his essay "Ideology as a Cultural System," in David E. Apter (ed.), *Ideology and Discontent* (New York: The Free Press of Glencoe, 1964), pp. 46–76.

terminal period of colonialism, European administrators and policy-makers had become concerned with economic, social, and political modernization. Yet, this could be viewed almost as a sort of liberal luxury to be indulged in above and beyond the more fundamental tasks—the maintenance of political order and of financial soundness. Any new achievement—the building of a road, the opening of a school, a slight increase in rice production, the registration of a few voters—was evaluated from the point of view of the past state of affairs; by definition these achievements constituted evidence of satisfactory progress. They hoped there would be more of it but seldom used the standards of modernity set by the world of industrialized nations to define the goals of government. Furthermore, they knew well that the territories over which they ruled were recent amalgams and so long as there were no very great disturbances, there was little concern with the growth of a sense of nationality; it would be incongruous to find in the report of a governor to the Minister of Colonies a discussion of the progress of "nation-building" or "national integration" in his territory. The tasks of government were manageable; there might be setbacks, but never any occasion for despair.

The outlook of their African successors is very different. Although it is questionable whether the population of the developing countries has truly undergone a revolution of rising expectations, there is no doubt that their *governments* have. Like colonial officials, African nationalists knew that their countries were poor. Now, however, they acquire great piles of statistical reports issued by international organizations which demonstrate, according to the cruel yardstick of per capita income and other quantitative indexes, that they are at or near the bottom of the universal scale of sovereign states. The difference is as sharp as that between a man's knowing that his skin is darker than that of another man and suddenly discovering that he himself is a Negro. Unlike colonial officials, Africans accepted this and other yardsticks as criteria against which their achievements must be evaluated; hence they undertook to bring about a fundamental change in the situation through governmental action. Similarly, relatively peaceful coexistence between disparate tribal groups within a recently created political container cannot be satisfactory for a new *nation;* there must be "national integration," measured against even more complex universal criteria. The absence of disturbances is not a sufficient indication that authority exists; a large proportion of the population must positively acknowledge its loyalty to the regime.

Strains arise not only because the new rulers adopt more burdensome goals and perceive problems differently, but also because new problems indeed arise around the time of independence. With the politicization of primordial loyalties, discussed in the last chapter, there are more indications of disunity than ever before; it may even appear that the country is less united at the time of independence than it was a decade earlier. Furthermore, to the extent that both the colonial regime and the national movement have been successful in bringing about institutional transfer, there is an increased awareness of the importance of the central authorities, and hence more demands are directed at them. There are few filters for these demands; the social habits that made the leaders very approachable before they became officials are not easily unlearned. The opportunity to participate in politics and administration has opened up the floodgates of claimants. At the same time, with all these new burdens, governments must shoulder the added expenses of sovereignty and accomplish all this with a relatively new and inexperienced civil service. At worst, precisely when they become aware of how much is to be done, the leaders are like an executive who frantically pushes the battery of buttons on his desk only to discover that the wiring is non-existent.

Further problems stem from the changing international system. Colonial officials tended to be highly suspicious of the activities of their counterparts across the border, a habit which can be traced to the European scramble for Africa; on the whole, however, each colony (or group of colonies) was part of a political system dominated by a metropolitan power. Concerns with neighboring countries were usually not important for African nationalists; at one level they were dealt with in terms of general aspirations for continental brotherhood and at another they often internalized the European attitudes. With independence, however, a West African subsystem came into existence. Neighbors often turn out to be strangers with similar aspirations but with different habits and often opposing interests, owing to competition for regional prestige, for the same scarce imported capital resources, and for the same markets for exports. Ghana and the Ivory Coast have been at odds since 1957; whatever the causes that led to the breakup of French West Africa into eight independent territories, there was, at least for a time, an exacerbation of territorial nationalism defined in opposition to one's neighbors. This contributed to the sense of crisis and growing insecurity. The countries that spoke a "revolutionary" language around 1959 saw themselves surrounded by a sort of Holy Alliance, the French Community; the members of that group viewed the former as dangerous beachheads of subversion and revolution.

Beneath all this there was another concern, seldom explicitly expressed. All Africans were brought up within a political order built by what were initially the most powerful nations in the world, an order which had existed for over half a century. Although they fought against it, it constituted the familiar order of things and supplied appropriate reference points. During independence ceremonies, political leaders must surely have meditated on how easily they had been able to alter the immutable *ancien régime* through their own efforts. But if they could do this with the relatively meager means they used, could not anyone else challenge the order they were creating as well? This lack of bearings and the over-all sense of insecurity enable us to understand the feelings behind statements that otherwise appear unpersuasive. "We must act promptly and boldly. The threat of danger makes it impossible for us to hesitate or temporize, even for a minute," exclaimed one minister at an international conference in 1959.[9] However much they might disagree with other Ghanaian pronouncements, most African leaders would firmly endorse as their own a statement the government made in a White Paper of 1962: "The strains experienced by an emergent country immediately after independence are certainly as great as, if not greater than, the strains expressed by a developed country in war time."[10] And the Ghanaians in turn would agree with President Houphouet-Boigny, who said, quoting Goethe: "I prefer injustice to disorder: one can die of disorder, one does not die of injustice. An injustice can be repaired."[11]

As Clifford Geertz has indicated, "It is a confluence of sociopsychological strain and an absence of cultural resources by means of which to make (political, moral, or economic) sense of that strain, each exacerbating the other, that sets the stage for the rise of systematic (political, moral, economic) ideologies."[12] Faced with the changing orientation of government and the disappearance of the organizing principles of political life provided by the colonial regimes, and ob-

---

[9] A. Adande, in Herbert Passin and K. A. B. Jones-Quartey (eds.), *Africa: The Dynamics of Change* (Ibadan: Ibadan University Press, 1963).

[10] Ghana, *Statement by the Government on the Recent Conspiracy* (Accra: Government Printer, December, 1961).

[11] *Fraternité*, September 13, 1963.

[12] Geertz, p. 64.

sessed by their own inadequacies, African leaders needed suitable concepts of political organization, categories, ends and means. What is a nation? How can it be built? How does one develop? "Ideology" is a way of thinking out loud about these questions, a way of creating order out of chaos, not only for the sake of the leaders themselves but also to provide a map for their countrymen. Through this process African polities can acquire an identity that is more real than the one which has been granted to them by legal fiat. Africans can overcome a sense of being mere political things manipulated by others. As Geertz has put it, "It is through the construction of ideologies, schematic images of social order, that man makes himself for better or worse a political animal."[13] Beneath a great deal of cant and much borrowed discourse, it is thus possible to detect an act of creation.

THE CASE OF GUINEA

Within West Africa it was in Guinea that the process of ideology-formation was initially most clearly visible. This can be attributed to a chain of circumstances which begins with Sékou Touré's political apprenticeship in the ranks of the *Confédération Générale du Travail* (CGT), the Communist-oriented French labor organization, from which much of his rhetoric and his great concern with ideology itself is derived. Under his leadership the PDG, which became a government party while still in the midst of its initial organizational spurt, initiated more fundamental changes than any other *Loi-Cadre* government from mid-1957 on. During the year that followed, Sékou Touré chose the more radical alternative on almost every political issue discussed in French West Africa; each of these debates provided another occasion to elaborate the party's ideology. Ultimately, through a process that is still not entirely clear, Sékou Touré's impetus led him to a showdown with General de Gaulle and to the decision to campaign for a negative vote in the Referendum of September, 1958, on the issue of the French Community. It is difficult to grasp in retrospect the depth of the crisis that followed: within a few days, unlike any other African government at the time, the Guinean leaders were left wholly to their own devices. They were fully self-conscious of their unique situation and felt the full impact of cultural strain in the face of an uncertain future.

---

[13]*Ibid.*, p. 63.

Hence, they took great pains to draw up a message which was then relayed and disseminated through the efforts of sympathetic French-speaking African intellectuals and especially the men of *Présence Africaine*. Within a short time several volumes of *pièces de circonstance*, speeches, Congress documents, and government programs appeared; many commentaries and English translations followed.[14]

The availability of these materials contributed enormously to the creation of a widespread impression that the Guinean régime was distinctive in that it *had* an ideology, and to the equally widespread assumption that there were corresponding fundamental structural differences between this and other new polities in the region. Although these were exaggerated conclusions, as we shall see later on, the fact remains that the process of ideology-formation is particularly visible in this case. In the analysis that follows, however, we must remember that in Guinea like in most other new states, political thought is usually not formulated by professional philosophers or other contemplative men, but rather by practical politicians. It is not expressed in the form of carefully wrought treatises but rather in the form of addresses to announce, to explain and justify particular choices of policies. Since the process of writing in an orderly, academic way about ideology involves bringing together themes that have appeared in scattered sources and in different contexts, there is always a danger of creating an impression of systematic thought where such a characteristic is in reality absent.

The basic concern, throughout Sékou Touré's published speeches, is the achievement of unity. The basic ideological paradigm emerged very early. In a speech delivered in January, 1958, when there was still a chance of achieving an interterritorial coalition, Sékou Touré referred to "the current of political unity which affirmed itself powerfully in all the territories" before the RDA Congress in Bamako of September, 1957, and stated that "this current must be grasped and brought to its natural outcome." He explained why this was necessary: "On the African plane, without political unity, colonialism will be beaten with difficulty, because it will seep into the cleavages that exist among Africans by exploiting internal contradictions of our societies, jeopardizing and increasingly postponing their disappearance." The remedy is simple: "It is therefore necessary to use all means to unite African

---

[14]These works include *Guinée: Prélude à l'Indépendance* (Paris: Présence Africaine, 1958); Sékou Touré, *Expérience Guinéenne et Unité Africaine* (Paris: Présence Africaine, 1962), and Sékou Touré, *La Guinée et l'Emancipation Africaine* (Paris: Présence Africaine, 1959); see also Immanuel Wallerstein, "The Political Ideology of the P.D.G.," *Présence Africaine*, XII, No. 40 (1962), 30–41.

parties into a single anticolonialist front and for African progress."[15] Similarly, within the territory, the current of unity that has arisen has enabled the leaders

> from the ward and the village to the territorial level, passing through the *cantons,* the *cercles,* and the regions, to regroup all good wills, all healthy energies, finally all the men and women whose rise to consciousness and courageous action is at the basis of the radiance of our Party.[16]

From these statements it is clear that Sékou Touré believes that (1) there is a natural trend toward "unity"; (2) African societies *are* divided; (3) these divisions are not to be viewed, as an American thinker might, as a healthy "pluralism," but rather in a negative way as "internal contradictions" (a Marxist borrowing); (4) unity is manifested in support for the dominant party. A corollary follows naturally from these four. Sékou Touré pointed out that the unity of Guinea was demonstrated in 1957 in spite of attempts by "enemies" to "sabotage" it. Hence, we may add: (5) the failure of unity can stem only from the actions of men who willfullly interfere with the natural course of history.

From this scheme, developed throughout the months and the years in other speeches, there emerges a conception of the political community. Some criterion of membership is necessary if a community is to have any significance, but in Guinea most criteria familiar to us from history are inadequate. Race, in its broadest sense, is too wide; it does not differentiate between Guineans and other Africans. In another sense, it is too narrow because it corresponds to particular ethnic groups; thus, Sékou Touré stressed that the most important task of the state was

> the definite reinforcement of the Nation by means of the elimination of the sequels of the regional spirit and all racist tendencies. How can the unity of the Nation be forged if there remains in the political and electoral domain irrational elements to be exploited or which can influence a part of Society? How can we insure that everyone will rapidly lose the myth of his race to the benefit of his identity as an African?[17]

---

[15] Sékou Touré, *Expérience* . . . , pp. 32–33.
[16] *Ibid.*
[17] *Ibid.*, p. 258.

Language poses the same problems as ethnicity: there is none that is Guinea's alone. Religion—in this case Islam—would encompass a large proportion of the population; but it would conflict with the secularist spirit of many of the leaders. Territory has relatively little meaning in a country whose boundaries have recently been defined by alien rulers. To the extent that nationalism must define a membership unit in which the participants share a political fate, it is not surprising to find the Guineans stressing the widest, best-known membership group, the party. The community is thus defined in partisan political terms. Support for the party and its ideas is a way of entering into a social contract, of participating in a community that is in the process of becoming.

As a community, the party is not exclusive. "Membership," as we have seen in the previous chapter, is defined vaguely and involves primarily non-involvement in another *political* organization. Unity is thus defined essentially in a negative way, the absence of opposition. Opponents can join and are invited to do so. Sékou Touré generously appealed to "our brothers BAG and Socialists," but asked them to surmount their "self-love, complexes, rancor, selfishness and jealousy," thus implying that they are not merely individuals who disagree with the party on legitimate grounds, but rather that they are morally defective.[18] If they want to become good men, they must join the party which, by implication, is thus defined as the *moral* community. This quality was stressed when, after a new election had consolidated the PDG's majority, Sékou Touré hailed its most recent adherents by saying "Here, allow me to solemnly salute all those men and women who, having definitely abandoned the path of sabotage and of crime, have recently joined us in our exalted task of the construction of a new Guinea."[19] After independence, the PDG viewed itself as the moral spearhead of all of Africa: "We must know that our political task now goes beyond the borders of Guinea. Our party becomes that of all Africans who love justice and freedom."[20] Having initiated this new order of things, Guinea must live up to its responsibility; unity must be maintained at all costs; once nation-building has been undertaken in the limelight of world publicity, no opposition can be allowed to interfere with the task of national mobilization.[21]

The basic paradigm of unity was extended to encompass the entire

---
[18] *Ibid.*, p. 32.
[19] *Ibid.*, p. 54.
[20] *Guinée: Prélude* . . ., pp. 167–68.
[21] *Ibid.*, p. 173.

set of institutions. Concerning representation, for example, Sékou Touré explained in a speech commenting on the new constitution shortly after independence that "fortunately, Guinean society is not divided into social classes with fundamentally opposed interests. The Constitution must favor a harmonious evolution of our Nation and it is in this sense that it provides for only one Assembly."[22] Futhermore, division of the country into electoral districts was abolished and all members of this Assembly were to be elected at large. This device is useful to suppress opposition, as we shall see in the next chapter, but it also has a symbolic meaning: to divide the country into districts suggests that the nation is composed of discrete and distinct parts; if it is defined as *one,* there is no reasonable ground for such differentiations. Sékou Touré commented:

> We could therefore only raise the mode of election of the representatives to the level of the Nation by instituting constitutionally the election of Deputies on a national list. Indeed, a Deputy must be mandated by the Nation as a whole and have no other concern than to better serve the national interests without allowing himself to be influenced by considerations of region, of clan, race, or religion.[23]

Once again, all possible cleavages are defined as illegitimate.

With all other voices defined out of existence, the people can speak only through the party. It must be prominent and supreme because "it, alone, represents the hyphen that binds all layers of the population, all those who, in the name of the population or of the party, are invested with even minimal responsibility."[24] The people are one; acting through the party, which directs the state, they build the nation. The party is the basis of the legitimacy of all other institutions; ultimately it *is* the people, it *is* the nation. Therefore, it must be one.

SPREAD OF THE ONE-PARTY IDEOLOGY

The major themes of the one-party ideology of Guinea were rapidly echoed elsewhere with local variations. It is difficult to determine whether there were genuine intercountry influences at work or

---
[22]*Expérience,* p. 258.
[23]*Ibid.*
[24]*Ibid.,* p. 362.

whether the concepts were re-invented autonomously in each case because they corresponded to a common situation. Within a short time, almost every leader had formulated his own version, almost as if the ownership of such an ideology was a matter of prestige akin to the possession of a national airline. In addition, African statements on the subject flowed at an increasing rate in response to the critical commentaries made by outsiders to which we referred in the introduction. In Ghana, for example, a series of articles began with "I do not agree with those political theoreticians and theoretical politicians who would want us to believe that it is wrong for all the country to belong to one party, and that an opposition is necessary in a democracy. . . ."[25] Less bluntly, Julius Nyerere wrote in the same year: "To minds molded by Western parliamentary tradition and Western concepts of democratic institutions, the idea of an organized opposition group has become so familiar that its absence immediately raises a cry of 'dictatorship.'"[26] It is not out of the question that these minds included Nyerere's own and that by setting forth the one-party argument he and other Africans were trying to silence their own nagging consciences.

An interesting illustration of this sort of interaction, which also elucidates some major patterns of thought, occurred in 1959 during a conference on representative government held under the sponsorship of the Congress for Cultural Freedom in Ibadan, Nigeria.[27] It was a unique occasion because although there had already been some pan-African conferences in Ghana the previous year, this was the first time that politicians and intellectuals from various African countries met with some non-African scholars and journalists to discuss politics informally. In spite of efforts by the organizers to cover a variety of subjects, ranging from international affairs to the civil service, the question of the one-party state rapidly dominated and spread like wildfire from formal plenary meetings into workshop sessions and private conversations in bars, tourist buses, and dance-halls. The initial spark was a paper presented by Professor David Apter on oppositions in new states. In order to enhance the persuasive quality of his argument, Apter avoided stressing the right of opposition to exist on philosophical ground but focused instead on its usefulness

---

[25]Quoted in Paul E. Sigmund, Jr., *The Ideologies of the Developing Nations* (New York: Praeger, 1963), p. 193.
[26]*Ibid.*, p. 197.
[27]Most of the papers were included in Passin and Jones-Quartey, *op. cit.* In addition, I am relying on my own manuscript notes.

from the point of view of the regime. "A political opposition," he stated, "is neither a luxury nor a danger. If it performs its functions well, it can be of crucial service both to the government of the day and to the people of a new nation."[28] Distinguishing between "values" —fundamental beliefs about what is right and wrong—and "interests" —more instrumental concerns and immediate desires—he urged political groups to oppose on interest grounds only, exercising discretion, discipline, and self-control.[29] Under these conditions, he explained, if it is allowed to operate, the opposition will provide a safety-valve for discontent, "information" which the government needs if it wishes to avoid sitting on a powder keg, and useful alternatives to government policies.

The distinction between "values" and "interests" is sometimes unclear even in a settled country where fundamental values are firmly anchored; in Africa, as the Guinean delegate pointed out in response to Apter's plea, opposition parties cannot be constructive precisely because there *is* disagreement on fundamentals between them and the ruling party. Democracy does exist inside the dominant party, but, he argued, the existence of an opposition party can jeopardize it because of fears that open discussion would provide ammunition for the enemy. Alexandre Adande of Dahomey, a country where the one-party state has never been successfully achieved, stressed the danger of *any* argument in favor of opposition: "Some people are consciously or unconsciously playing into the hands of a hard-pressed imperialism when they frighten us with the scarecrows of dictatorship, fascism, neo-fascism, totalitarianism, and so on, simply because we have decided to bring our conceptions into line with reality." He too stressed that "history teaches us that a colonial and underdeveloped country can win and consolidate its independence, if not by the creation of a unified party, at least by the establishment of a common front of all live forces," citing Morocco, Tunisia, Ghana, and even Nigeria, where independence had to be preceded by agreement between Azikiwe and Awolowo, as evidence. For Adande, political parties were essentially evil because beneath their idealistic appearance, they "actually represent a definite class or a definite economic interest"; by defending special interests, they shatter the general interest.[30] Pinto, another

---

[28]David E. Apter, "The Role of the Political Opposition in New Nations," in Passin and Jones-Quartey, p. 57.
[29]*Ibid.*, p. 66.
[30]Quoted *ibid.*, pp. 71–77.

Dahomeyan, confirmed that opposition exists only to provide its leader with jobs; a Togolese warned that "too much freedom kills freedom, too much democracy kills democracy," and Patrice Lumumba prophetically preached union "because divisions lead to the suicide of Africa."[31]

A debate even arose over the sense of the meeting. When the Nigerian *Daily Times* announced that the seminar as a whole preferred the one-party system, the Nigerian chairman of the seminar issued a counterstatement: "This report is seriously misleading. . . ." The dominant view of African speakers, he said, was that "while it was important that the Opposition should be constructive, the existence of an Opposition was necessary."[32] My own impression is that this was incorrect; among Africans at the conference, only some of the Nigerians deviated from the major trend. Furthermore, in spite of the cordial atmosphere, the conference provided a good illustration of the problem at stake; given differences over fundamental beliefs, agreement to disagree on "interest" issues could not be reached.

One press report, which stated that there was a major difference of opinion between French- and English-speaking Africans on the one-party issue, drew attention to an interesting question.[33] It could indeed be suggested in 1959 that the one-party ideology was peculiarly "French," perhaps because party pluralism, associated with the ineffective Fourth Republic system, could be dismissed without difficulty; because the one-party ideology had some affinity with De Gaulle's plebiscitary democracy; and because France had shown less concern with the institutionalization of pluralism during the process of decolonization than Great Britain.

In the then newly created Federation of Mali (Senegal and Sudan), the dominant parties retained their separate existence but formed the *Parti de la Fédération Africaine* with some affiliated minority parties in other French-speaking West African countries. On the occasion of the PFA's first congress, held in July, 1959, President Senghor of Senegal set forth his own variation of the one-party ideology. He distinguished initially between the state (or supreme government), which the Federation of Mali already was; the fatherland (*patrie*), constituted primarily by the ethnic groups to which the population belonged; and finally the nation, which unites fatherlands. The

---

[31]Manuscript notes of the conference.
[32]*Nigerian Tribune*, March 21, 1959.
[33]*Agence France Presse* dispatch to various newspapers.

nation, according to Senghor, is therefore not a given such as "the people"; indeed it can arise only as the result of conscious effort, an existential choice which enables men to escape from "natural determinants." Understandably, within the context of the Mali Federation, Senghor argued that the nation can be other than unitary; presumably Senegal and Sudan were to remain legitimate components at a level somewhere between that of fatherland and nation.[34] Within this scheme, the state is the means to achieve the nation and the party in turn controls the state.

Here, Senghor distinguished between "single" and "unified" parties (*parti unique et parti unifié*). While the monopoly of the single party is established by law (this was the case nowhere in Africa in 1959–60), in the regime ruled by a unified party, opposition is allowed to exist. But the concept is very ambiguous. On the one hand, Senghor acknowledged the legitimacy of opposition, stating that "opposition . . . must pursue the same goal as the majority Party. It is to prevent the crystallization of social groups into antagonistic classes. Its function is, very precisely, to be the conscience of governments and of majority parties." At the same time, however, he told the congress:

> While we must condemn the single Party, does it mean also that we must abandon the Unified party, i.e., the hope of rallying the Opposition to our national ideal? Nobody could sustain this view, nobody *does* sustain it in the P.F.A. . . . [35]

Furthermore, he warned that opposition is "tempted to serve foreign powers. . . . You know it, parties are teleguided [sic] from the outside. . . . Our duty is to prevent subversion." Not only must opposition be eliminated because it is a threat to the state but also because the unified party is a moral community: "It is because the stand of the P.F.A. is just that we can rally the Opposition to it." Elsewhere, the situation is different: in countries like the Ivory Coast (at that time the major antagonist on the issue of interterritorial federation), the opposition agrees with the PFA and thus has legitimate, moral grounds to oppose the dominant party. How, then, does Senghor's "unified" party differ from the "single" party? It is inclusive rather than exclusive, i.e., it attempts to incorporate its opponents rather than to elimi-

---

[34] Léopold Sédar Senghor, *Nation et Voie Africaine du Socialisme* (Paris: Présence Africaine, 1961), p. 25.
[35] *Ibid.*, p. 117.

nate them; but this, as we have seen, is also a characteristic of the one-party ideology of Guinea. Perhaps "unified" also acknowledged the division of the PFA into major components. In the final analysis, however, beyond saying that ours is a unified party, yours is a single party, little can be said about this distinction.

The ambiguity of the concept appears also in a statement by a Sudanese spokesman, Madeira Keita, a few months after Senghor's formulation and shortly after the opposition in Sudan had joined the *Union Soudanaise:*

> I used to say "single party," but I ended up accepting President Senghor's expression, "unified." French has many nuances and the word "unified" was adopted because the legal possibility remains to form other parties. We say "unified" because other parties, other political groups, sacrificed themselves voluntarily for the sake of unity.[36]

But then the speaker went on to use the two adjectives interchangeably, and his address was published under the title of "Le Parti Unique en Afrique"!

The remainder of Keita's argument resembles that of Sékou Touré. He begins with a historical review on the basis of which he argues that multiparty systems have negative consequences. First, regardless of their orientation on other issues, the governments of Senegal, Sudan, and the Ivory Coast were more stable than the coalition governments of Upper Volta or Dahomey. Second, political competitiveness served to divide Africans since leaders, in order to obtain offices, were forced to play up regionalism or "internal racism." Hence, only a one-party situation can insure stability, which in turn is needed to insure effective government, a "healthy situation," to limit corruption, to kill opportunism, and "in order not to provide means to our enemies, i.e., colonialism, which is anonymous, but which hitherto has had spokesmen for division in our countries." Not only is the one party necessary, but it is also a natural outcome which corresponds to what Marxists would call "objective conditions." Where they exist, parties represent classes or interests; and Keita argues that although there may be classes in Africa, there are no opposed interests since all agree on the major goal, the construction of a state apparatus for de-

---

[36]Madeira Keita, "Le Parti Unique en Afrique," *Présence Africaine,* XX (February–March, 1960), 19. Other quotations in this paragraph are from the same source.

velopment. There are no cleavages on which parties could be based—no differences of wealth, no religious problems. In the absence of these cleavages, he argues, political competitiveness was based merely on "opportunism," i.e., on individuals who wanted political office. In order to do this, leaders were forced to play up "regionalism" or "internal racism." This led to a "bad period of electoralism" which is now over because the people, who never understood why unity took so long to be realized, have finally prevailed over the leaders and hence "progressively the countries began to move toward the formula of the unified party."

Does this threaten democracy? Keita of course answers in the negative. First, there are some democratic regimes that have no parties (he does not specify which); but second, while the single parties of other countries might indeed be undemocratic, those of Guinea and Sudan are democratic because they are well organized and disciplined, and the leaders bow to the majorities in party councils. Under such conditions, there is not even any need for autonomous voluntary associations outside the party: "If the party is the true expression of the genuine aspirations of the people, if it is their spokesman, if it is the instrument for the realization of the State, there is no reason for the syndical organizations . . . not to be in harmony with the political formation."

In the early part of 1960, there were already tensions between Senegal and Sudan in terms of both interests and over-all ideological concerns; it is therefore significant that in speaking of democratic unified parties Keita included Sudan and Guinea, but left out Sudan's partner in the PFA, the dominant party in Senegal. And it is also significant that neither Senghor nor Keita raised the question of the nature of a unified party which included two components, the UPS (a merger of the old BDS and other groups over the years) and the US, each dominant in its own country. At any rate, neither Senghor's stress on the non-unitary "nation" nor these other considerations remained relevant once the Federation broke up. And although this event stemmed from many causes, there is no doubt that it was due to a considerable extent to the incompatibility of "federation" with the one-party, unitary tendency.[37]

Within French-speaking West Africa the Ivory Coast seems to

---

[37] See William J. Foltz, *From French West Africa to the Mali Federation* (New Haven: Yale University Press, 1965), which contains also an outstanding comparative analysis of the views of the Senegalese and Sudanese leaders in 1959–60.

occupy a unique position because although the PDCI achieved a political monopoly earlier than any other organization, none of its leaders, from President Houphouet-Boigny downward, has ever expressed himself in written form on the subject of the one-party ideology beyond a small piece in the party newspaper. Whatever the reasons for this deviation from the usual pattern—possibly the personality of the President, the desire to maintain a public image attractive to suppliers of investment capital, or perhaps the very success of the PDCI—it is erroneous to conclude that the Ivory Coast is therefore less "ideological" than Mali, Guinea, or Senegal, or even that it does not have an ideology.[38] Its ideology is simply less obvious than it is in some other cases, and we must look for it with greater care.

When we do so, it is not surprising to discover a familiar theme with local variations. The stress on unity can be traced back to 1946 and has been repeatedly re-asserted. In 1958, for example, President Houphouet-Boigny warned about the dangers of an "immoderate love of freedom or of democracy" and a few months later cryptically told elected officials "For the time being—and I am sure you know why I hope that this will last—the Ivory Coast is fortunate enough to have a movement that has gained a large majority throughout the country."[39] Much as Senghor did at about the same time, he specified that he was not against *any* opposition, but that opponents must agree to operate within the limits of stated fundamental issues, which included at that time the decision *not* to federate with other French-speaking countries and *not* to seek independence—precisely the issues on which opposition would naturally be expressed. We also find in the Ivory Coast a theme encountered in Guinea: not only is the absence of opposition an indication of unity, but *because* unity has been achieved, there is no reason for opposition to exist. Thus, the Minister of Interior, in answer to a question about future elections, indicated in 1961 that "given the achievement of unity," to have electoral competition would be undesirable; nevertheless, if in spite of this unity some parties wanted to compete, they could do so in 1965.[40]

The Ivory Coast ideology resembles the others in terms of its

---

[38] President Houphouet-Boigny's reluctance to commit his views to print might stem from the experience of the post-war period, when the RDA produced a number of pamphlets and manifestoes which proved embarrassing when its policies changed.

[39] Zolberg, *One-Party Government*, pp. 235, 261n, and 252–68, *passim*.

[40] *Fraternité*, June 9, 1961. This official's promise cannot be tested since he has himself been removed from the active political scene after alleged participation in a plot. There was no competition in the November, 1965, elections.

concept of conflict and cleavage. Ethnic and other primordial differentiations are not viewed as legitimate bases for the organization of political groups because they threaten the unity of the nation and impede progress toward modernity. As for socioeconomic cleavages, "We are lucky in the Ivory Coast that the colonizer has not willed us two classes"; hence there can be only one party.[41]

As we have already pointed out, the Ivory Coast seldom self-consciously discusses ideology. The only event which resembled the ideological seminars common elsewhere occurred in 1962. Defined as an institute devoted to the methodology of political action, it took on a distinctive local flavor. It was, appropriately, chaired by the secretary-general of the party and included government and party officials; but the guest star was a distinguished French professor of comparative government. The contents were less surprising. After nearly a week of lectures and debates dominated by the theme of the single party, the rapporteur of the first committee on "Institutions and Political Forces" indicated that "properly speaking, the PDCI in the Ivory Coast is not a single party, but de facto, a party alone [*un parti seul*]. This situation corresponds to a state of fact, the entire nation having brought its support to this party." In exchange, the party must represent the entire nation, not just privileged groups, and must bring about the political and democratic education of this mass. He concluded that the political regime of the Ivory Coast cannot fall into any prefabricated category but is genuinely original

> since, albeit under the authority of a man illustrious above all others, who governs with only one party, its institutions and especially its behavior are absolutely democratic, because political discussion is free and even encouraged, as well by the Chief of State as by the highest levels of the Party in the midst of which decisions are taken on the basis of majority rule.[42]

The Ivory Coast ideology does differ somewhat from the others in that, although the party claims to represent all the people, there is on the whole less of the populist flavor that prevails in Guinea or Mali. Furthermore, while the state owes its legitimacy to the party, the party owes its own increasingly to the Leader. These views have even been

---
[41]*Fraternité*, May 8, 1964; the same theme was sounded in many interviews conducted in 1959.
[42]*Fraternité*, January 26, 1962.

embedded in a textbook intended for civic education in the elementary schools. Differentiating among types of government, the author lists old-fashioned tyrannies; dictatorships (such as Hitler's Germany); monarchies (e.g., Great Britain and ancient Ghana); and democracies. The latter category, broad enough to encompass both the USA and the USSR, also includes the Ivory Coast which, however, "is fortunate enough to have only a single political party. This proves that all Ivoiriens are grouped around their leader and that they approve of him wholeheartedly."[43]

If it was originally "French," the one-party ideology did not remain so for very long. In Ghana authoritarian trends had been visible for some time and Bretton reported, on the basis of his 1956 observations, that "leaders in Government and Party . . . appear to be unanimous in their opinion that conditions in Ghana do not require an 'alternate government.' "[44] Nevertheless, it is true that as of 1959, the one-party ideology had not yet been fully formulated. Some of its features soon began to appear. In a major speech delivered on the occasion of the tenth anniversary of the founding of the CPP in mid-1959, President Nkrumah said,

> Comrades, it is no idle boast when I say that without the Convention People's Party there would be no Ghana, and that without political independence there would be no hope of economic salvation. The Convention People's Party is Ghana. Our Party not only provides the Government, but is also the custodian which stands guard over the welfare of the people.[45]

"The CPP is Ghana." This often-repeated phrase, with its companion slogan, "Ghana is the CPP," which appeared soon afterwards, is startling in its implications. "What *is* Ghana?"—or Guinea, or the Ivory Coast, for that matter—is more than a rhetorical question. Although in the course of achieving independence the Gold Coast took on a new name, this could have had little significance for most inhabitants of the territory; only some educated men, who had read the works of European historians and anthropologists or of a few American Negro writers, could have heard of the tenth-century kingdom of

---

[43]Ivory Coast, *Nation, Société, Travail: Manuel d'Education Civique* (Abidjan: C.E.D.A., 1961), p. 40.
[44]Henry L. Bretton, "Current Political Thought and Practice in Ghana," *The American Political Science Review*, LII (March, 1958), 52–53.
[45]*Speech Delivered by the Life Chairman on the Occasion of the Tenth Anniversary 12th June 1959 of the Convention People's Party* (Accra, no date), p. 4.

the Western Sudan, thousands of miles away. Even if the name were familiar, the question remains and must be answered if the nation is to take on a concrete meaning. The answer Nkrumah gave is the same as that provided by Sékou Touré; a fundamental clue to the understanding of the one-party ideology is contained within this simple equation.

In the same speech, tracing the history of nationalism, Nkrumah hailed the legitimate ancestors who manned the pre-World War II political groups, but damned the still-active immediate predecessors of the CPP as a "petty bourgeoisie." "These been-to's despised the common people and the common people distrusted them."[46] By contrast, the masses "recognized in the Convention People's Party the only hope for their salvation." As in Guinea, so in Ghana the party is a moral community and the struggle between the CPP and its opponents is described in appropriate terms: some of the people were led astray and "All the forces of darkness, feudalism, and ignorance joined together to stab the revolution in the back and rob our people of the fruits of their struggle on the very verge of independence." But the party successfully "met the challenge and once more the people rallied to its side." The triumph of the CPP marks a "political revolution," the result of which is "political power vested in the people." Nkrumah then made the identity of the people with the party, of the party with the nation, and the supremacy of the party over other institutions even more explicit through tangible arrangements:

> I want it to be known categorically and unequivocally that since the party forms the Government, the members of the Central Committee ... will in the future take precedence over non-Central Committee Ministers at all Party ceremonies and at all public and civic functions. I want it to be firmly understood that it is the CPP which makes the Government and not the Government which makes the CPP, and we intend to give public acknowledgement to this fact by raising the prestige of our Party to its proper status in our national structure.

Although the government took appropriate measures to insure the success of the 1960 referendum on the republican constitution, the

---

[46] *Ibid.*, p. 6. "Been-to" is a West African pun (on *Bantu*) intended to goad those who have studied abroad, who have "been to" England or America. Nkrumah, of course, is one of these. Other quotes in this paragraph are from the same source, pp. 6–19.

opposition was still allowed to participate. The campaign provided another opportunity to affirm party supremacy but the Ghanaian ideology still lacked the final commitment to the one-party concept:

> We are the Party of the workers, the farmers and all progressive elements in our community. . . . The CPP is a powerful force; more powerful, indeed, than anything that has yet appeared in the history of Ghana. It is the uniting force that guides and pilots the nation and is the nerve center of the positive operations in the struggle for African irredentism. Its supremacy cannot be challenged. THE CPP IS GHANA AND GHANA IS THE CPP."[47]

It was not until the results of the referendum indicated serious disaffection or indifference—Nkrumah obtained only about 16 per cent of the possible adult vote in the capital[48]—and further problems arose that the final step was taken.

In a series of articles that appeared in a new party organ in the spring of 1961, Koffi Baako acknowledged the right of criticism—not surprisingly, since President Nkrumah himself had recently severely castigated the CPP for its inefficiency and corruption—and the right to change governments by voting, but denied the right of organized opposition. The CPP "will not allow freedom to destroy freedom," he stated, echoing a familiar phrase. The remainder also gives us a sense of *déjà vu*:

> We believe that a monolithic party is necessary in an ex-colonial state which is inevitably faced with the task of correcting past maladjustment, years of neglect and of colonial mental conditioning, and of building a new, really independent, happy and proud state. Such a young state cannot afford to dissipate its national efforts through the senseless wranglings and obstructive and destructive tactics that organized political opposition encourages. Besides, it is through such opposition parties that colonialism and imperialism seek to perpetuate their hold on the country.[49]

---

[47]Kwame Nkrumah, *I Speak of Freedom: A Statement of African Ideology* (New York: Praeger, 1961), p. 209. Emphasis in the original text.

[48]Dennis Austin, *Politics in Ghana* (London: Oxford University Press, 1964), p. 391.

[49]Quoted in Sigmund, p. 194.

Although the Ghanaians completed the construction of their one-party ideology later than most other countries, they not only caught up with but eventually extended the theory two steps beyond their neighbors: they transformed the one-party concept into a legal rule by making of it a constitutional amendment; and furthermore, in a display of blunt honesty, they gave it a meaningful new name, Nkrumahism. Ghana is the CPP, but the CPP is the Leader.

CONCLUSIONS

The main theme of this chapter has been that there is a strong relationship between psycho-sociological and cultural strain and the one-party ideology. Before exploring the further implications of this proposition, I want to stress briefly three problems that stem from the preceding analysis. First, by concentrating almost exclusively on the one-party concept, I have left out of consideration many other views of West African leaders concerning the political, social, and economic worlds. In part this omission will be overcome in the following chapters when we examine in some detail the operations of the new regimes. Nevertheless, this remains a *partial* view of what can be called the total ideology of the West African states. It is partial in another sense as well. By discussing the views of leaders alone, we have remained at the level of "forensic" ideology, completely ignoring the more "latent" ideology of lesser actors in the political system.[50] Although this can be justified in terms of the topic of this book, this omission, stemming from total ignorance of the subject, prevents us from considering such important questions as the degree to which the leaders have been successful in creating a new political culture.

A second problem arises from the question, "To what extent are the views discussed here genuine?" Are they mere verbiage and rhetoric, mere "ideology" in the vulgar sense of the word? No responsible observer would claim that they are "genuine" in the sense of being accurate descriptions of political structures and processes; after all, the men quoted are politicians, not political scientists; hence we cannot use them to make inferences about the structural and processual aspects of the regimes in which these statements occur. But are they "genuine"

---

[50]This distinction is borrowed from Robert Lane, *Political Ideology* (New York: The Free Press of Glencoe, 1962).

in the sense of expressing fundamental *beliefs* about political life? Although many of these official pronouncements correspond to concepts that are enunciated in private informal conversations and methodical interviews, it is still possible that the latter are themselves staged for the benefit of journalists and visiting scholars. Hence the strongest argument in support of their genuine quality stems from their consistency over time and the striking degree to which the views of leaders from different countries who are at odds on many other issues reinforce one another.

This brings us to the third problem, the question of similarities and differences. Some of the differences among the five states considered can be attributed to local circumstances and to the background of the individuals concerned. Thus, Ghanaian political language is a mixture of Protestant-evangelical, Marxist, and British parliamentary modes of expression, often combined with a flashy style and a popular invective which stem from the fact that in Ghana, as in no other country discussed in this book, there is an indigenous newspaper culture which goes back to the nineteenth century. Whatever Ghanaians may say, it is always sure to be more colorful and vituperative than whatever is said in Senegal, where the principal spokesman is an *agrégé de grammaire* and a writer of French poetry who has long been associated with refined French intellectuals. There is no literate tradition in Guinea to compete with that of the left-wing French trade-union milieu in which Sékou Touré grew up politically; hence, whatever is said there is sure to sound much more purely "Marxist" than what one hears elsewhere. While the Ivoiriens shared in this tradition to some extent, they have in later years become very business-minded, going so far as to entrust, until recently, the publication of their party newspaper to Frenchmen working in Paris; one would hardly expect a Ghanaian tone in *Fraternité*.

Thus, although there are important differences in the orientations of these leaders in other fields such as economics and international affairs, they share a common view of the process of national integration, of the meaning of unity, of the duties of rulers and citizens, and of the role of political conflict. It does not appear very useful to distinguish between the "monistic model" of Nkrumah, Touré, or Keita, and the "pluralistic model" of Senghor or Houphouet-Boigny.[51] The

---

[51]Charles Andrain, "Democracy and Socialism: Ideologies of African Leaders," in David E. Apter (ed.), *Ideology and Discontent* (New York: The Free Press of Glencoe, 1964), pp. 157–69.

most significant difference in political outlook concerns the relationship between party and government. The notion of partnership is always present, but the stress varies from the more extreme notion of party supremacy initially found in Guinea and Mali, to the almost opposite relationship in the Ivory Coast, where leaders have stated at times that the party must be an instrument of government, with Ghana and Senegal somewhere in between. To what these differences can be attributed is difficult to determine. We can resort to the particular circumstances of decolonization, but these are themselves partly the result of different orientations, and the explanation surely does not apply to Ghana. Given the overwhelming importance of personal leadership in all five countries, there may be no alternative to an understanding of the personalities and backgrounds of the men formulating the ideology, a goal which we cannot achieve given the present state of our knowledge of these men.[52] Whether these differences have important consequences is another question, however, which can be answered only by examining the operation of the respective regimes. Meanwhile, we can speak of a generalized "one-party ideology" for these five states.

If ideology is a conceptual map created by men facing an unknown political world, what are its connotations and implications? The stress on the party is easily understood since from the point of view of the leading political actors, it is the only trustworthy institution available. It is not a strange import, like governmental bureaucracies; it is not something that has been constructed by others for a different purpose. They built it, they are familiar with its operations, and it benefits from a sense of tradition and familiarity. To rely on the party for almost everything that needs to be done is an attempt to turn the future, for themselves as well as for the population, into a continuation of the recent nationalist past. The party is also the only available large membership association; it was a concrete expression of the "nation" long before many men knew that their fates had become linked because they lived together within certain territorial boundaries.

The shift we have stressed, from "party-dominant" to "party-alone," is a significant indication of the nature of the concept of "unity" which prevails in West Africa. During an earlier phase, the desire to achieve a dominant position was justified *in terms of instrumentalities*—the need to prevent one's opponents from taking over, the

---

[52]Another relatively unexplored possibility is the traditional political culture. For some hypotheses concerning this factor, see Morgenthau's chapter on Mali in Coleman and Rosberg, especially pp. 223–25.

need for a united front in bargaining situations, the need for governmental stability. Increasingly, however, the existence of a single party has become an *expression* of unity. While to other men, living in a more stable environment where there is less fear that things will fall apart, "unity" can be and often is viewed as a process of interaction between a variety of parts (e.g., *e pluribus unum*), under conditions of great stress such as those which prevail in West Africa, unity requires "oneness." In the presence of many signs, however repressed, that primordial loyalties remain strong, that individuals are concerned with short-term satisfactions rather than with long-term national goals, it is necessary to create and to maintain at all costs *one* stable indicator of unity: the single party. Thus, unity becomes objectified, tangible. From having been a means, the political monopoly becomes a self-justifying *goal*.

The importance of political "oneness" links the West African one-party ideology with some familiar historical moods, and particularly with that of the Jacobins. In their search for unity, *"volonté une,"* Robespierre and Saint-Just were unprepared to recognize a representative assembly as embodying the general will because by definition parliament is controlled by vested interests—much as many Africans are unprepared to view parties and factions as anything but selfish. For the Jacobins, the general will did not even reside in a majority, but rather the majority was where the general will resided, even if that will happened to be expressed by a numerical minority. The people must speak—*"Vox Populi, Vox Dei"*—but they must vote well; however, because they are still bearing the scars of oppression, recorded opinions do not reflect the true will of the sovereign. Ultimately, the general will spoke through Robespierre.[53]

Both for the Jacobins and for many African ideologues, oneness also involves a strong stand against internal "federalism." Because in American political thought this concept is associated with a centralizing tendency, it must be remembered that in the European tradition, "federalism" has retained the opposite connotation. For the Jacobins, the "Fédérés," provincial activists who led insurrections in major French cities in 1793, were "immoral," subversive of the unity of government, and assimilated to the "wicked rich" and counter-revolutionaries.[54] Although in Africa there is sometimes a more positive

---

[53] J. L. Talmon, *The Origins of Totalitarian Democracy* (New York: Praeger, 1960), pp. 115–16.

[54] *Ibid.*, p. 55. For the connotations of "federalism" in French-speaking Africa, see Foltz, pp. 63–68.

sense of "federalism," related to Pan-Africanism and superterritorial unity, there is no doubt that even the strongest partisans of larger political communities, such as Ghana, view internal "federalism" or political decentralization of any sort much as did the Jacobins. There is little need to stress the obvious points that the notions of separation of powers and of checks and balances are incompatible with the mood of "oneness" for much the same reasons.

Going one step beyond the manifest stress on the single party and on oneness, it is possible to detect an overwhelming concern with the avoidance of conflict, with rationality, and with order. In order to make these points clearer, it is useful to examine a parallel ideological tendency in the domain of economics. When, in advocating socialism at the beginning of his autobiography, Kwame Nkrumah states as his justification that "capitalism is too complicated a system for a newly independent nation," he is voicing a belief which is as widespread as the one-party concept itself.[55] In an article which appeared before such statements became so commonplace as to be almost entirely unnoticed, Francis X. Sutton drew attention to the overwhelming faith African leaders had in the possibility of rational control of the economic environment and in planning.[56] One might add to this the connotation suggested by Nkrumah's statement that the notion of self-adjusting market mechanisms, operating through a "hidden hand," is genuinely foreign to most African thinkers. This is indeed not surprising; faith in the beneficial outcome of processes that even economists admit are "models" which do not correspond to tangible reality can be sustained only through a repeatedly favorable outcome, a condition which is clearly not met in Africa. But why should one think that planning is less "complicated" than market mechanisms? It must be because such a procedure is more parallel to the normal way in which a fairly educated man proceeds to confront everyday situations; furthermore, this notion is in keeping with the faith in reason Sutton stressed, which is reinforced by the newness of its acquisition as a concept, resembling the enthusiasm for the Goddess Reason associated with the French Revolution.

The parallel of the plan is helpful when we consider that in most

---

[55] Kwame Nkrumah, *Ghana* . . ., p. vii. See also my article, "The Dakar Colloquim: The Search for a Doctrine," in William H. Friedland and Carl G. Rosberg, Jr. (eds.), *African Socialism* (Stanford, Calif.: Stanford University Press, 1964), pp. 113–27.

[56] F. X. Sutton, "Planning and Rationality in the New African States," *Economic Development and Cultural Change*, X (1961).

of Africa planning is not viewed as the provision of certain self-adjusting mechanisms, credit controls, discount rates, etc., which even the USSR is beginning to adopt, but rather as a fairly simple, mechanical, and clock-like contraption, one which consists of visible levers and gears and which can be manipulated by relatively educated and intelligent men, thus enabling them to control the future. Paradoxically, it is also evident that these plans cannot possibly serve such utilitarian purposes because they are usually completely unrealistic, both in terms of means available and goals to be attained, and are based on minimal information concerning the economy. We can infer therefore that they are intended not only as instruments, but also as reassuring and tangible *symbols* of rationality, control, and order.

The plan is more than a mere analogy; it reveals in a different sphere the latent structure of the one-party ideology. The notion that political conflict—even in the orderly form of electoral competition and interacting group pressures—will bring about the general good in some mysterious fashion, or that the clash of ideas will bring about the truth, is as alien and inspires as little faith in Africa as the self-adjusting market mechanisms of capitalism. Politics can and must be planned, as much as economics. This is feasible because the leaders view themselves as rational, and it is necessary because order must prevail. The one-party ideology and its concomitant unitary notions together form "guided" or "planned" democracy. The levers and gears must be as visible as they are in the plan; hence the proliferation of institutional mechanisms which we shall discuss in the chapters that follow.

There is another implication in this type of thought. If one believes that a system is mechanical, then any stoppage is the result of the intrusion of extraneous elements; any economic or political disturbance is the result of interference by outsiders, subversion, or sabotage. Who these willful "counterplanners" may be varies from system to system, depending upon their orientation; but it is characteristic that most African leaders resort to cabalistic thought to account for obstacles or failures; here it is "imperialism" or "neo-colonialism"; there it is the "yellow peril" or "freemasonry," much as others who share this mode of thought elsewhere speak of "Wall Street" or of the "Communist conspiracy in Washington."[57] In the face of great insecurity, there is an ever-growing restriction of the area of dissent, not

---

[57]The dynamics of cabalism are analyzed by Lane, pp. 113–30.

only because the dissenters sometimes constitute a real threat, but because the very possibility of their existence is disturbing.

Thus, the one-party ideology has shifted from an instrumental orientation to a self-sufficient one in which certain symbols take on very great significance. As a map of the political world, it provides relief from strain even if reality differs greatly from the formulations it contains, as we shall see it does. Much the same can be said about economic ideology and plans, but the advantage of political ideology is that it is the one thing that African leaders can construct without external expert help. In the creation of this map Africans are involved in an activity which closely resembles a religious ritual, in a more profound sense than the one in which many have spoken of Communism as a "political religion."[58] Political ideology becomes an incantation which genuinely transforms reality, even if nothing else happens, by changing men's view of it. "In the beginning was the Word." African leaders hope that these words will create life, that the one-party concept will be transformed into national unity, into effective authority, into an orderly state. They hope that some day, the Word will be made flesh.

---

[58] My use of the term "political religion" owes much to, but differs substantially from, Apter's. See "Political Religion in the New States," in Clifford Geertz (ed.), *Old Societies and New States* (New York: The Free Press of Glencoe, 1963), pp. 57–104.

CHAPTER III

THE ACHIEVEMENT OF UNANIMITY

EQUIPPED WITH THE IDEOLOGICAL MAP DEVISED BY THE LEADERS OF THE West African states, we can now better follow the manner in which they transformed their regimes. A quick check-list of the steps involved, by now a monotonous recitation of well-known political facts, must include the following: co-optation, intimidation, exile, or detention of political opponents; modification of the electoral system to make competition impossible or at least unlikely; transformation of the constitution inherited from the European tradition to give wide discretionary authority to the executive and to restrict the activities of representative assemblies; the use of a criterion of political loyalty to select key administrators and division of the country into satrapies; administrative control over local government; reduction of the independence of the judiciary or creation side by side with it of dependable political courts; transformation of major voluntary associations into ancillary organs of the party or their political neutralization; control over written and radio communications; reduction of consultation within the party and of accountability of the leadership to the members, while stressing the physical existence of the party by multiplying headquarters, branches, and committees; institutionalization of adulation of the paramount leader or, alternatively, concentration of all effective authority in the hands of a few men while using the language of collective leadership.

For the sake of convenience we shall distinguish within this overall transformation two major aspects: the attempt to achieve unanimity by erasing all traces of political opposition and the attempt to create a new institutional order by modifying the party and the government. Although it is often difficult to place a particular event in one or the other of these two categories since it may be inextricably related to both processes in the minds of the leadership and in its consequences, we shall deal with them separately in this chapter and in the next.

OPPOSITION: GROUPS AND ISSUES

Although we are primarily concerned with examining the behavior of the rulers of the West African party-states, it is impossible to understand why they behave as they do unless we view their acts as a response to certain types of situations, i.e., as part of a process of interaction between the rulers and their various opponents. Since we have so far been concerned primarily with the incumbents, it is necessary to consider briefly the characteristics of their opponents.

At first sight the observer of the West African political scene may well be struck by the variety of obstacles the rulers of different countries have encountered: Senegal has never been faced with anything like the Ashanti problem experienced by Ghana, and Ghana in turn has never had to deal with the left-wing student opposition that seems to be characteristic of many French-speaking African states. Although reliable generalizations must await further investigation of the social, cultural, and economic "environments" of the political systems under consideration, there are certain identifiable regularities in the *sources* of opposition which stem from common sorts of differentiations found among the countries of the region.[1]

(1) Where there has been a long history of African political participation, as in Ghana or Senegal, some members of the older generation of nationalists have not adapted to the changing times and especially to what is from their point of view the uncouth aspect of mass politics. Although their very outlook militates against obtaining a mass following of their own and hence from seriously threatening the regime, they are prestigious figures and often retain a small but loyal personal following of individuals of their own generation. If they choose to resist incorporation in the ruling group they can sustain themselves for a relatively long time. The best known case in this category is that of J. B. Danquah of Ghana, founder of the United Gold Coast Convention, who continued to speak out for many years against such measures as preventive detention and on such issues as

---

[1] My use of "environment" in relation to the political system is based on David Easton, *A Framework for Political Analysis* (Englewood Cliffs, N.J: Prentice-Hall, 1965), Chapter V, pp. 59–75.

republicanism.[2] Although he was himself repeatedly detained, this did not prevent him from continuing to preside over the Ghana Bar Association and to hold occasional public press conferences, until he died during a last period of detention. Lamine-Gueye of Senegal falls into this category as well. Although his party merged with the dominant one, Lamine-Gueye and some of his followers retained a certain autonomy within the *Union Progressiste Sénégalaise* (UPS) and are known to have disagreed with other leaders on some important issues. Groups of this type are faced with an ideological problem: much of their criticism of the regime is inevitably voiced from the point of view of norms and values which stem from the colonial past or from Western European politics. What to an outside observer appears as "liberalism" becomes "reaction" in the eyes of members of the ruling party. Because they are also weak organizationally, they provide highly convenient and vulnerable targets for attack by an insecure regime.

(2) A second major category of opposition groups are organizations led by political entrepreneurs who base their claims on primordial solidarities, mainly ethnic. How these arose and persisted was discussed in Chapter I, and we need not repeat this discussion here except to stress that *all* political organizations in Africa, including the dominant parties, have such ethnic components, and hence that what differentiates the ins from the outs in this respect is that the outs, in seeking an organizational base from which to challenge the ins, cannot but stress particularistic appeals.

Beyond such general statements, is it possible to suggest under what conditions ethnic parties arise? Certain typical patterns are discernible. In almost every African country the capital tends to become a sprawling metropolis in which the majority of the inhabitants are recent arrivals from fairly distant regions. The original natives of the city and of its surrounding area (very often a tribe which claims ownership of a major part of the land on which it is built), such as the Ga around Accra, the Lebou of the Dakar area, the Ebrie of

---

[2]Information concerning political events which are described and analyzed in this and the next chapter is drawn, unless otherwise indicated, from the following periodical sources: for Ghana, *West Africa* (London); for the Ivory Coast, *Fraternité* (Abidjan); for Mali, *L'Essor* (Bamako); for French-speaking Africa generally, *Afrique Nouvelle* (Dakar), all for the period 1957–65. In addition, *Africa Digest* (London), *Chronique Politique Africaine* (Paris), and *Africa Report* (Washington) contain useful summaries of events in the countries under consideration. It is inevitable that some of the information also be drawn from a multitude of conversations with Africans during my own visits to Africa and theirs to the United States.

Abidjan in the Ivory Coast, or the Soussou of the Conakry region, tend sooner or later to feel overwhelmed by the recent immigrants, who are often more enterprising than they are, and to vent their resentment toward them in the form of political opposition. This is particularly disturbing to the regime because politics in the capital is highly visible both to its inhabitants and to outsiders, especially peripatetic newspapermen.

Groups of this type may or may not coincide with another type of group, usually the tribe or tribes which were among the first to undergo colonization and in whose midst the first capital was established. The Cape Coast Fanti in Ghana, the population of Kayes in Mali, the Agni and *lagunaire* groups around Bingerville, Grand Bassam, and Aboisso in Eastern Ivory Coast, and the people of Saint-Louis in Senegal had the initial advantage of greater access to education and to modern occupations than others and also of greater prestige in European eyes than the remainder of their countrymen. Although it was often from their midst that early generations of leaders arose, they were often not able to retain control of the nationalist movement for reasons already discussed in (1) above. At the same time these groups continue to manifest a certain political pretension based on their high position within what can be considered an inter-ethnic system of social stratification.

At the other end of this stratification system, political discontent often arises among groups who for a long time were considered by Europeans—and eventually by their compatriots who internalized these European views—as "primitives." In countries where Islam is dominant, they are sometimes groups which remain "pagan," such as the Dogon, some Bambara, Senufo, and Minianka of Mali; elsewhere, especially in coastal countries, they are usually groups located in the north or in the heart of relatively inaccessible tropical rain-forest zones, such as the Bété of Western Ivory Coast. *Because* they were considered to be "primitives," they often had much less access than others to various modernizing influences and hence really did become relatively more backward. But by the end of the colonial period enough change had occurred to produce in their midst political champions who in turn aroused ethnic solidarities even where they had never existed before.

Another source of ethnic opposition stems from culturally distinctive groups who accidentally straddle two or more countries. When this occurs, at least one part of the larger group comes to believe that it is in the wrong country. The most famous cases in this category are those which became international problems by virtue of the existence of trusteeship agreements, such as the Ewe of Ghana and Togo. But almost every country has groups of this type, and their feelings of separation from the remainder of their fellows became exacerbated when the very process of independence stressed national boundaries. Thus, there was much more annoyance in the Kayes region of Mali *after* Senegal and Sudan became separate countries than before, just as there was among groups in Eastern Ivory Coast and Western Ghana. A very similar phenomenon occurs in relation to the readjustment of *internal* administrative boundaries: for example, a minority ethnic group in a given district or region commonly wishes to be reunited with other members who constitute the dominant ethnic group of another district or region. Such issues are known to be important sources of conflict in countries such as Nigeria and Uganda, where they are obvious because the definition of the components of the federal state were legitimate questions openly debated. These issues are much less visible where they are defined as administrative questions and did not enter into the constitutional process before independence; nonetheless, they are equally important sources of ethnic discontent.

Another variable related to the appearance of ethnic opposition is the traditional political system of the group as modified by a particular system of colonial rule. It is fairly obvious, for example, that an ethnic group which had a well-differentiated state system before European conquest and which was administered under a system of indirect rule would be likely to survive as a politically relevant unit within an independent African state. If for some reason that group is not sufficiently large or well enough located strategically to dominate national politics, it would tend to act as an opposition group. But in spite of some stimulating hypotheses formulated by Apter and Coleman on this subject, there has been to my knowledge no systematic data-gathering and therefore I cannot make precise suggestions concerning the importance of this variable.[3]

Ethnic opposition is highly disturbing to the regime on several counts: the desire to maintain separate sub-identities is always at odds

---

[3] See in particular David Apter, "The Role of Traditionalism in the Political Modernization of Ghana and Uganda," reprinted in William John Hanna (ed.), *Independent Black Africa* (Chicago: Rand McNally, 1964), pp. 254–77, and James S. Coleman's section on Africa in Gabriel Almond and James S. Coleman (eds.), *The Politics of the Developing Areas* (Princeton: Princeton University Press, 1960), pp. 258–60.

with the Jacobin spirit of "oneness" discussed earlier; because it involves preserving traditional authorities such as chiefs or councils it is "unmodern"; any talk of territorial readjustment is clearly "treason" and "separatism." Furthermore, although when opposition manifests itself it is almost always possible to find an ethnic (or related "primordial") dimension, this dimension is never the only one involved; it is usually accompanied by specific political and economic demands for a more equitable distribution of national income (if the group happens to be relatively less fortunate) or for the retention of a greater share of income produced in the region under some federal or quasi-federal arrangement (if the group happens to be more fortunate). In the one case, the group interferes with the allocation of scarce resources determined under the Plan; in the other, it is being selfish. Finally, opposition based on primordial solidarities is also the most difficult to control since it feeds on itself.

(3) Although it is not very useful to speak of socio-economic "classes" in Africa because differentiations are very recent, often visible within one generation only, and there is as yet little evidence of intergenerational transmission of status in the modern sector, certain categoric groups stand out as sources of political opposition based on education, occupation, and source or amount of income. They include especially civil servants; railroad, harbor, and construction workers; and cash-crop farmers. In most African countries civil servants (including low-level clerical government employees) constitute, from the point of view of government, one of the most demanding groups in the society. On the whole, because of their very occupation and training, they have internalized to a greater degree than anyone else the views and the style of life of their European predecessors, including a desire for substantial comfort and contempt for politicians. Almost everywhere, they feel that on the grounds of native ability and training, *they* are qualified to rule, rather than merely to execute the policies of others. There is some variation from country to country. In Ghana, where it is more appropriate to speak of a British-trained African civil service, many of its members are more educated than politicians and have internalized the British liberal-bureaucratic outlook; they can be thought of as constituting a permanent but relatively latent "rightist" opposition to government. In French-speaking Africa the upper ranks of the civil service were much less open to Africans; the politicians themselves were often government employees and there is therefore little social differentiation between the present governments and

the civil service. But the government employees formed the bulk of the trade-union membership and developed an acute "grievance" orientation toward their employer, the colonial government; this was later transferred to the new government and exacerbated by the feeling that they have been betrayed by their erstwhile colleagues, who have now acquired a "bourgeois" spirit. Hence, civil servants in French-speaking countries tend to constitute a more active, but also more "leftist," opposition.

Although there has been relatively little industrialization in most of these countries, all of them have railroad lines, harbors (if on the coast), and fairly important construction enterprises (government and private); in Ghana and Guinea there are extractive enterprises (mines). The manpower needs of such economic activities tend to create relatively large agglomerations of workers in certain towns or in neighborhoods within the towns. Although labor unions are often very loosely structured and fragile, such patterns of human ecology tend to facilitate rapid communications among the workers and enable them to act as visible mobs. It is relatively easy for them to make trouble for their employer; and since their employer often happens to be the state, their behavior is politically threatening.[4] Strikes under such conditions inherently constitute a challenge to state authority and hence merge into sedition; demands for higher wages easily upset current budgets and developmental plans because personnel expenditures usually constitute the largest single component of governmental costs; furthermore, the government believes that an inflationary spiral of wages jeopardizes conditions required to attract external capital investment.

In almost every West African country, the pattern of colonial economic development has insured the emergence of one major cash crop grown for export by numerous African farmers located in a particular region of the country: cocoa in Ghana, coffee and cocoa in the Ivory Coast, peanuts in Senegal and in Mali. For reasons we cannot go into in very great detail, the international prices of these commodities tend to fluctuate widely; hence in the past, African farmers had very insecure incomes, a common source of agrarian discontent

---

[4]This stress on the political role of trade unions in Africa takes issue with propositions contained in Elliott J. Berg and Jeffrey Butler's chapter on this subject in James S. Coleman and Carl G. Rosberg, Jr., *Political Parties and National Integration in Tropical Africa* (Berkeley and Los Angeles: University of California Press, 1964), pp. 340–81. A careful reading of Berg and Butler suggests, however, that they used "political" in a much narrower sense and that the evidence they cite in fact supports the proposition I have advanced here.

which often led to the sort of agitation discussed in Chapter I. On the whole, colonial governments had begun to cope with these fluctuations by multiplying market controls on production and price. Not only has this approach been continued by the successor states, but they have tended to use market controls to secure substantial resources, i.e., as taxation. Whether or not such measures are justified occasions much debate among economists; from our point of view, it is sufficient to point out that under such a system economic demands by farmers are necessarily political, much like wage demands for white-collar and industrial workers. But in addition, as we pointed out earlier, just as an economic component often accompanies ethnic opposition, so an ethnic dimension is often found within agrarian discontent because of the regionalization of cash-crop development. Thus, although there are many cocoa-growers in Ghana who are *not* Ashanti and many Ashanti who are *not* cocoa-growers, Ashanti nationalism and demands for better cocoa prices or opposition by farmers to certain conservative measures have been inextricably inter-related.[5]

(4) As Lucian Pye has noted, "The non-Western political process is characterized by sharp differences in the political orientation of the generations," primarily because of "a lack of continuity in the circumstances under which people are recruited to politics."[6] In most West African countries it was relatively easy for a particular age-cohort to move from relatively modest positions in the occupational structure to the highest political positions; within a single decade, clerks and elementary school teachers became cabinet ministers. But for the next generations, whose expectations are based on the experience of their predecessors, conditions have fundamentally changed. First of all, the uppermost positions have already been filled by relatively young men who see no precise time-limit to their tenure. Second, men with some education and occupational qualifications rapidly became relatively less scarce because of the huge growth of secondary and higher education during the postwar decades. Thus, the supply has increased manifold while the demand has abruptly decreased; the result is that newer generations face an insurmountable glut which frustrates their aspira-

---

[5] On this subject and for Ghana in general during the period under consideration, see in particular Leo Snowiss, "Democracy and Control in a Changing Society" (Master's thesis, University of Chicago, 1960); and Larry Bowman, "Agrarian Group Development in Ghana" (Master's thesis, University of Chicago, 1964).

[6] Lucian Pye, "The Non-Western Political Process," in Harry Eckstein and David E. Apter, *Comparative Politics* (New York: The Free Press of Glencoe, 1963), p. 660.

tions. To these discrepancies in political recruitment we may add gaps in political socialization. The regime has on the whole very little control over the major mechanisms of socialization, the educational structure and the family: the first has inherited the norms that prevailed during the colonial period; the second has been probably least affected by social, economic, and political change and hence remains very traditional. There is therefore little likelihood that new generations will have a set of attitudes compatible with the requirements of the new order.

The claims of youth in its various forms are particularly intolerable because many African societies place some importance on age as a criterion for political authority; although, traditionally, young men often had an institutionalized place in the system, it was strictly defined and was not allowed to interfere with political control before authoritative roles were vacated by the death of their incumbents. Although many of the present officeholders themselves at one time or another spoke in the name of the right of youth to participate in politics—in Ghana, this is true not only of the founders of the CPP, but also of *their* predecessors!—they now tend to view themselves as elders confronted by impatient successors. The stress the incumbents had earlier placed on educational qualifications in order to challenge more traditional leaders is now a source of embarrassment to them because on the basis of such criteria the new youth is often better qualified than they are. The solution often takes the form of a general denunciation of "impractical intellectuals" who are ungrateful, know nothing about the realities of the country, and did not have to sacrifice the best years of their lives to the anti-colonial struggle.

The behavior of the youth itself contributes to the intensity of intergenerational conflict because their dissatisfaction and opposition often take such irritating forms as refusal to return home after studying abroad for many years at the expense of their own government or the wholesale condemnation of the incumbent generation. The latter phenomenon is related to the tendency for youthful discontent to be manifested not only in individual deviance from prevailing norms but also in the appearance of age-homogeneous movements and organizations, functional equivalents of the familiar youth gangs of industrialized societies.[7] Although, as we shall see in the following chapter, the

---

[7] Conditions under which the phenomenon occurs are specified by S.N. Eisenstadt, *From Generation to Generation* (Glencoe, Ill.: The Free Press, 1956).

regime often attempts to co-opt such groups by the institutionalization of "youth wings," the youth organizations tend to maintain in their own midst a distinctive subculture and to act autonomously in the political sphere.

* * *

Although this consideration of sources of opposition does not enable us to determine when, in what form, and with what degree of intensity a specific latent group will become activated and challenge the regime, it does help us to understand certain characteristics of the interaction between the regime and its opponents. In the previous chapter it was suggested that the dominant party was unlikely to subscribe to the notion that opposition groups could have constructive roles to play in the new order. Now it can be seen that in fact the characteristics of the opponents themselves give support to this view because the opposition is led, almost necessarily, to challenge fundamental values. Like the incumbent leaders, challengers tend to view political conflict as an all-or-nothing proposition. Human and physical resources are so limited that any disagreement over their allocation becomes a major threat. The game of politics is so new that the rules have not yet been internalized and there can be little or no agreement on them; indeed, none can be taken for granted. Factors which might make for the limitation of issues are almost non-existent. Whether it begins by asking for better wages or better prices, whether it is dissatisfied with the delimitation of constituencies or with lack of consideration for generational claims, the opposition almost always ends up challenging the entire order which the regime is dedicated to build.

This absence of restraints is not limited to debate over issues, but affects other forms of behavior as well. It is also unfortunately true, as the leaders charge, that opposition rapidly gives rise to violence. Even normal electoral competition arouses latent cleavages that create open and violent conflict within or between communities. This is due to the absence of cross-cutting affiliations within communities; when conflict occurs, it rapidly involves individuals as whole men and entire communities.[8] Whatever the intent of the CPP and the National Lib-

---

[8] I have discussed this process in greater detail in *One-Party Government in the Ivory Coast* (Princeton: Princeton University Press, 1964), pp. 4–7, 77. There, as here, my analysis is based on Georg Simmel, *Conflict* (Glencoe, Ill.: The Free Press, 1955); James Samuel Coleman, *Community Conflict* (Glencoe, Ill.: The Free Press, 1957); and Lewis Coser, *The Functions of Social Conflict* (Glencoe, Ill.: The Free Press, 1957).

erations Movement (NLM) in Ghana between 1954 and 1956, there is no doubt that there was much violence in Ashanti during this period; in Guinea there were bloody riots involving the pro-PDG Malinke and the anti-PDG Soussou in and around Conakry around 1958, as there were between two groups of Bambara descended from different dynasties in the Segou region of Mali between 1958 and 1960. The Ivory Coast also has a record of violent clashes between political opponents in several regions. Strikes and other forms of economic protest which often involve violence in other countries are equally likely to do so in West Africa and to have even more disruptive consequences for the economy because of the smallness of the total system.

Africa has also had its share of political assassination in recent years: besides the death of Lumumba, which was a major shock to the entire continent, there was within West Africa the almost accidental killing of the President of Togo, Sylvanus Olympio, the several attempts on the life of President Kwame Nkrumah, and a number of much less publicized successful and unsuccessful attempts in other countries. Many of these fears were confirmed by what is, from the African point of view, an almost unbelievable event, the assassination of President Kennedy. Beyond this manifest level, however, there prevails in most of West Africa another source of fear which is difficult to discuss seriously without appearing to stress sensationalism. Most African leaders—whether of dominant parties or of opposition groups —keep a solid foot in their own traditions, especially in the intimate sphere of the occult. The widespread belief in magic, divination, and geomancy is accompanied in most cultures by a belief in the power of witches to act on an individual at a distance. It is not an exaggeration to suggest that the atmosphere of fear noted in village life prevails even in what are in other respects modern political circles.[9] Ultimately, therefore, opponents may constitute a violent threat even if they have no obvious political power.

A third source of growing tension is the involvement of opposition groups in extra-national politics. In the case of youth, for example, it is evident that students from underdeveloped countries are usually courted

---

[9] For the political importance of such factors in traditional political systems, see in particular Paul Bohannan, "Extra-Processual Events in Tiv Political Institutions," *American Anthropologist*, LX (1958), 1–12. A very interesting account of the village atmosphere is contained in Elenore Smith Bowen (Laura Bohannan), *Return to Laughter* (London: Gollancz, 1954). See also the specific incident related below.

by opposing major powers. It matters relatively little whether they are wholeheartedly "pro-Western" and "liberal," such as the Ghanaian students who went so far as to testify against their own government before a subcommittee of the United States Senate, or vociferously revolutionary and "anti-Western," as is much more commonly the case in French-speaking Africa: whatever their orientation, students tend to respond with irresponsible enthusiasm to the flattering advances of foreign governments and hence tend to give support to the charge of disloyalty that is often hurled against them.[10] More generally, after independence, members of opposition groups in one country were often welcomed as political refugees in another one which had a different political orientation, as has been the case with Ivory Coast refugees in Guinea or Ghana, Ghanaians in Togo or in the Ivory Coast, Malians in Senegal, and vice versa. The situation is sometimes paradoxical, as when the Agni who sought to preserve their traditional political system in the Ivory Coast were welcomed in Ghana, where the regime was in the process of attacking their kinsmen, the Ashanti, on the very same grounds. These refugees tend to allow themselves to be used by their hosts in propaganda campaigns directed against their own country; even if this were not the case, their very presence in an antagonistic foreign country appears to confirm the ruling group's claims that the opposition, as Senghor expressed it, tends to be "teleguided" from the outside.

OPPOSITION: TECHNIQUES OF SUPPRESSION

We now turn to the other side of the interacting systems, the actions of the dominant party in dealing with opposition. Because in much of the scholarly and journalistic literature on Africa some countries are more notorious than others in this respect, it is important to note at the outset that the local circumstances which accounted for differences in ideological jargon, as was pointed out in the previous chapter, also account for differences in over-all political style and even for the quantity of effort expended to reach the goal of unanimity. The consequences of this fact are somewhat paradoxical.

---

[10]See the publication, "Ghana Students in United States Oppose U.S. Aid to Nkrumah," *Staff Conferences of the Subcommittee to Investigate the Administration of the Internal Security Act and Other Internal Security Laws of the Committee on the Judiciary United States Senate* (Washington, D.C.: Government Printing Office, 1964).

Let us imagine, for example, that the government of country A, in an attempt to get some opponents out of the way, brings charges against them under existing laws, only to find that the judiciary has retained its own norms and refuses to recognize the validity of the charges. The government might therefore pass a law providing for the detention of these opponents without trial, then another law declaring certain of their past activities a crime, bring charges, and entrust the whole affair once again to the courts. If the judges come up with what is, from the point of view of the government, an undesirable verdict of acquittal, the executive replaces them with more sympathetic men, who finally declare the opponents guilty. All of this is reported in the local government-controlled press. From the point of view of observers accustomed to detecting authoritarian trends on the basis of violations of public liberties, such as an international commission of jurists, country A is guilty of having adopted an *ex post facto* law and a bill of attainder, of having violated the principle of independence of the judiciary and the right of habeas corpus. They travel to country B and are happy to find no bad laws on the books and judges whose tenure has not been disturbed since independence. In the conclusions of their report, country B is cited as an example which country A would do well to imitate. What they do not know, however, and what their procedure could not uncover, is that the government of country B has also eliminated its opponents, but has done so with more discretion. A group of party militiamen arrested them and kept them incarcerated in a private house; later, they were punished by a specially constituted party tribunal which was dissolved immediately afterwards. Little publicity was given to the whole process because country B is very conscious of its "image" abroad. Paradoxically, then, in reality country A has displayed a greater concern with the rule of law than country B! Thus, unless an attempt is made to compare broad patterns rather than collections of discrete events, misleading conclusions concerning differences between regimes might be drawn.

Why countries A and B chose different means to achieve approximately the same goal may stem in part from different legacies from the colonial era. Although the example above is somewhat exaggerated for the purpose of illustration, it does correspond to an important distinction between Ghana, on the one hand, and most of French-speaking Africa on the other. Although Apter was overly optimistic in viewing the Gold Coast as a successful case of institutional transfer of parliamentary democracy, he was correct in stressing that British norms generally had begun to take root in the Gold Coast.[11] Hence the implementation of the one-party ideology in Ghana has been a more complex process, reflecting obstacles stemming from the norms internalized by the leaders themselves as well as by significant groups in the society. In addition, issues concerning freedom of the press and academic freedom, for example, have arisen there to a much greater degree than in French-speaking Africa because at the time of independence Ghana was unique in that it did have a press and a genuine university. Finally, as we saw in Chapter I, the opposition in Ghana had also come much closer to resembling the dominant movement than any other in the countries under consideration; more effort was required to eliminate it from the political scene. For all these reasons, to which we must add the fact of greater publicity, there is much more evidence of authoritarianism in Ghana than in any other West African country. But this does not necessarily mean that if regimes are compared *in toto,* Ghana is in fact more authoritarian; paradoxically, the opposite may well be the case.

With these remarks in mind, we can now proceed to a consideration of two sets of techniques which illustrate particularly well the dominant party's approach to the achievement of unanimity: the first pertains to the electoral system, the second to political justice.

ELECTIONS

Almost everywhere, elections have been so manipulated as to insure control by the incumbents over political recruitment. The overall trend has been first merely to reduce the opposition's chances of success at the polls, then to control all candidacies, and finally to obtain the appearance of unanimity by means of a government-administered plebiscite. The length of time taken to reach this goal and the particular methods used to achieve the desired result have varied somewhat from country to country.

French-speaking Africa understandably moved fastest and farthest in this direction because of the French colonial tradition of managed elections, which had culminated in the referendum of September, 1958, with overwhelming majorities previously unheard of in any of the countries involved. Afterwards, as was mentioned earlier, Guinea adopted an original system of elections by transforming the entire

---

[11]See David Apter, *The Gold Coast in Transition* (Princeton: Princeton University Press, 1955, 1959) and *Ghana in Transition* (New York: Athenaeum, 1963), *passim.*

country into a single constituency with simple majority and list voting, in a manner closely approximating the American method for choosing Presidential electors within a single state. Regardless of the distribution of the vote, this system insures that all the seats will go to the victorious party. Although Guinea originated the system, the Ivory Coast was the first to put it into operation, moving from 60 assembly seats and 19 constituencies in 1957, to 100 seats and 4 constituencies in 1959, and finally to 70 seats and a single constituency in 1960. Although in both 1959 and 1960 the constitution specifically provided freedom for the organization of political parties, nobody challenged the PDCI in either year, because the consequences of opposition were well known. Furthermore, the party developed a clever technique for dissuading potential candidates from filing independently. Its own nominees are not made public until a few minutes before the deadline; hence, hardly anyone with even the slightest chance of obtaining a place on the dominant party's ticket would jeopardize this chance by betraying his uncertainty and impatience; and when the PDCI ticket is finally made known and some find that they are not on it, there is no time to consult with other individuals willing to take an equal chance. Guinea used the same system in 1963, and Mali in 1964. In all three cases recorded results were similar: almost 100 per cent participation in the Ivory Coast in 1959, 1960, 1965, and in Guinea in 1963; in Mali a jump from a 32 per cent turnout in 1959 (when the opposition was still active and obtained 24 per cent of the votes cast, but not a single seat) to an 88 per cent turnout and the usual unanimity for the single slate of candidates in 1964, when, because of a discrepancy in population figures used by different ministries, the total number of persons announced as having voted (by the Ministry of the Interior) was greater than the Ministry of Planning's own estimate of the total adult population.[12]

Senegal has moved in the same direction but more hesitantly. Elections were quite free in 1959 and only partially restricted in the regional elections of 1960 and the muncipal elections the following year. It was not until the major crisis of December, 1962 (to be discussed in the next chapter), posed a serious threat to the regime that Senegal adopted plebiscitary electoral methods. Although the opposi-

---

[12]More precisely, the official figure on voters was 2,130,000 (out of 2,419,054 registered); the estimated population age 21 and over was 1,927,940 (computed from population figures in *Annuaire Statistique 1963 de la République du Mali* [Bamako, May 1964; mimeographed], p. 1).

tion was still allowed to campaign in February, 1963, it labored under very severe official difficulties and the vote for President Senghor was nearly unanimous. The single constituency system was established under the new Constitution of 1963 and implemented in the elections to the National Assembly later that year; for this election, unlike those in Guinea, Mali, or Ivory Coast, however, an opposition list was constituted. There were violent clashes during the campaign and this relative liberalism was tempered by the arrest of the opposition's secretary-general; his party obtained only about 5 per cent of the votes cast. Finally, when municipal elections were held in early 1964, the opposition did not bother to challenge the UPS candidates.

Ghana followed a much more tortuous path and took even longer to institute full-scale one-party plebiscitary elections. At the Parliamentary level, the CPP began with a majority of 72 out of 104 seats in 1957. By the end of the Parliament's first year, 5 members of the opposition had crossed the floor and 2 who had been imprisoned were replaced by CPP members in by-elections. Later, others were arrested, some fled in anticipation of arrest, and yet others boycotted Parliament in protest; the CPP then passed a new law stating that their seats would be declared vacant if they failed to attend sessions; by-elections were held and although until 1960 the opposition contested most of them, the CPP won a monotonous succession of victories. By the time of the 1960 Presidential election, held in conjunction with a referendum on the republican constitution, the CPP had secured 88 of the 104 seats.

The Presidential election, scheduled to take place over three days, marked the major turning point. When, after the first-day results in Accra indicated, as we saw previously, that the turnout was low and that the opposition had made a good showing, the government expended much effort to insure that results elsewhere would make up for Accra. Turnout in the remainder of the country was indeed much higher and the opposition's share much lower. The final tally indicated that nearly 90 per cent of the participants had voted for Nkrumah and the draft constitution; but total participation was still only 54 per cent, a far cry from the results that were being routinely announced in French-speaking Africa by this time.[13]

The CPP then continued its drive in Parliament, whose tenure had been renewed without an election for five more years, and whose

[13] Dennis Austin, *Politics in Ghana* (London: Oxford University Press, 1964), p. 394.

membership was increased to 114 with the addition of 10 special women's seats. The opposition no longer contested by-elections, and by the time Parliament was finally dissolved in 1965, the CPP had obtained 108 out of the 114 seats. A full-scale plebiscite was held in 1964 to ratify the constitutional amendment declaring Ghana to be a one-party state. On this occasion the total vote was more than twice as large as in 1960; 2.7 million were recorded on the "yes" side and only 2,452 on the "no." Perhaps because of this satisfactory result, there was no attempt to stage a repeat performance and elect an enlarged Parliament in 1965. Following the British practice for uncontested elections, all 198 CPP candidates were simply declared elected; under the new constitutional provisions they then re-elected the President.

POLITICAL JUSTICE

Ghana is the only country so far to have written the one-party state into law; yet most others, while preserving freedom to organize parties in their constitutions, have multiplied effective legal measures to prevent their appearance. A common sort of rule, which Ghana has also adopted, is the one which prevents the formation of any organization devoted to ethnic or other forms of "particularistic" propaganda: in effect, given the necessary nature of opposition groups, this makes most of them illegal by definition. Formally or informally, all the countries have also resorted to expulsion or deportation to eliminate some opponents: as early as 1957, Ghana began to deport some foreign Africans charged with participation in opposition politics and also moved undesirable individuals from one part of the country to another; in 1959 after repeatedly warning a labor leader not to resist efforts to organize a single government-minded union for civil servants, the Ivory Coast loaded him on a truck and deposited him near the border of Guinea; in similar cases in Ghana and elsewhere it almost seems that individuals have been given a choice between self-exile or arrest.

Although it is well known that an increasing number of persons have been detained, it is impossible to compare the records of different countries in this respect because some publicize their actions while others do not. Much more is known about Ghana in this as well as in other respects because in spite of all, Ghana, as we have already suggested, has retained a greater sense of rule of law. In 1958, a number of politicians were arrested and charged with sedition; when found not guilty by a Ghanaian court, the government pushed through parliament a Preventive Detention Act, enabling it to hold individuals without the usual legal procedures. It was still possible at that time (1958-59) for the opposition to challenge the validity of some of the arrests under PDA; the courts voided some of them and individuals were re-detained.

The special character of Ghana clearly emerges from the fact that in 1960 the opposition was able to obtain consideration in the courts of its charge that the PDA was illegal because it violated the right of habeas corpus. And although the courts did not agree, arguing on proper British constitutional grounds that Parliament is sovereign, and hence that any law is legal, the Chief Justice did express the hope that the law would be modified. Instead, however, coercive measures were stepped up in the face of ever-growing insecurity. After the government uncovered a first attempt to alter the regime by violent means (1959), new laws were made to facilitate the fight against conspiracy and subversion and to prevent the circulation of "false news." By the end of 1960, the government admitted that 118 people were being held under PDA. Following a major strike in Sekondi-Takoradi in 1961, there was a new wave of arrests, followed by bomb explosions in Accra.

In a White Paper on the political events of 1961, the Ghana government defended PDA by arguing that however undesirable such a law might be as a part of the permanent system of government, strains were very great, and normal procedures were ineffective because individuals known to be guilty were able to escape prosecution. Furthermore, the government believed that during the difficult years after independence, the letter of the law should not be enforced; preventive detention was therefore a human alternative to prosecution under charges of treason or sedition, making "ultimate reconciliation" easier.[14] Following this, PDA was amended so as to eliminate the provision for automatic release at the end of the stated period; new laws were passed making statements ridiculing the government or the state a crime; and a special court, composed of the Chief Justice and two other regular members of the judiciary, was created to deal with crimes against the state.

Trends were not clear at the beginning of the following year, 1962. On the one hand, the CPP seemed to be undergoing a purge, in which pressure was stepped up against a number of its own leaders, such as

---

[14] Ghana, *Statement by the Government on the Recent Conspiracy* (Accra: Government Printer, December, 1961), p. 34.

Gbedemah; on the other, there appeared to be a certain relaxation of coercion against opponents outside the party. It was announced at midyear that about half of those held under PDA were being released, including J. B. Danquah, who promptly assumed leadership of the Ghanaian bar and publicly condemned all the new coercive laws. The mood changed after a first open attempt to assassinate the President, in August, followed by two more before the end of the year. Coercive measures were stepped up once again and shortly before it was due to expire in 1963, PDA was renewed in spite of some opposition by CPP members in Parliament. Even then, however, a number of detainees were released.

The first group of individuals implicated in the 1962 attempted assassination were brought to trial under the special court and found guilty: five received the death penalty, and two others lesser sentences, in April, 1963. A second trial of five persons charged with conspiracy to commit treason *and* with treason, including two former cabinet ministers, began shortly afterwards. Although it was held before a special court, the trial was public and lasted fifty-one days, with the accused having full right of counsel. In December, 1963, the court announced that two had been found guilty and were sentenced to death, but that three others had been acquitted.

Clearly caught by surprise, the government kept the three under detention while the Chief Justice was dismissed. The tempo was stepped up again: a new assassination attempt, the constitutional amendment making Ghana a one-party state, a law making organized opposition treasonable, another providing that the President can dismiss judges, and once again the detention of J. B. Danquah, who died in prison. New judges were appointed to the Supreme Court and after a new months-long trial, this time closed to the public, it was finally announced that the three men formerly acquitted had been given the death penalty. In addition, a new law specified that obviously guilty persons cannot go free because of mere errors in trial procedure on the part of the prosecutor or the judge. Immediately afterwards, however, the President announced that the three death sentences had been commuted to imprisonment for 20 years, and following his re-election in 1965, 100 individuals under detention were amnestied. So far, there is no indication that *any* of those who received death sentences have been executed.

The Ghanaian pattern of increased coercion combined with alternative periods of reconciliation is typical of the entire region. Most other countries actually created special political courts much earlier and removed them completely from the province of the regular judiciary. In 1959 Guinea reformed the administration of justice "to avoid procedural dodges"; the following year, a special political court composed of members of the *Bureau Politique,* of the National Assembly, and of party wings, functioning behind closed doors, became operational; it was used again following another plot in 1961. A similar procedure was followed by Mali to prosecute nearly one hundred people allegedly involved in a plot to sabotage its new currency in mid-1962; several death sentences were meted out, but they were also changed later to life imprisonment. It was announced in mid-1964 that the two principal accused, prominent leaders of the former majority party and ex-Ministers of the Fourth Republic, had died in detention under strange circumstances.[15] Most of the small fry detained in 1962, however, were released or given reduced sentences on the anniversary of independence in 1965.[16]

Lest the impression prevail that such procedures are peculiar to countries that speak a more revolutionary language, it is important to consider the cases of Senegal and the Ivory Coast, where on the whole the government has carefully maintained a judiciary administered mostly by French magistrates and under only slightly modified French legal codes and procedures. As in the case of elections, so in the case of the judiciary the Senegalese regime is mildest. A special political court was created in 1961 when a French magistrate released one of the regime's opponents; it became operational a year later, following the announcement that a plot, allegedly directed from Mali, had been uncovered. It meted out sentences of up to 20 years, several of them in absentia. Following the Senghor-Dia clash of December, 1962, a special court composed of members of the National Assembly, patterned after the American tribunal for impeachment, was created. Dia and five co-defendants were brought before it in 1963, but with the full benefit of French and Senegalese defense counsel; Dia himself was allowed to testify publicly on his own behalf and proceedings were not interrupted when he provided his own interpretation of the events, stressing

---

[15] The first official explanation was that they died of an illness; the second, that they had been shot when the truck in which they were being transported was ambushed by a Tuareg band north of Timbuktu. However strange, the latter explanation may well be true, because its publication was embarrassing to the government, which was forced to admit the existence of a Tuareg uprising many months after they had announced that it had been put down.

[16] *L'Essor,* October 4, 1965.

the full implications of his own involvement, but justifying it on constitutional grounds. He received the maximum sentence of life imprisonment, while others were given lesser ones. The opposition leader arrested during the 1963 electoral campaign was brought to trial a year later and received only a two-year sentence. He benefited from executive clemency in 1965; the plotters of 1962 had received a general amnesty in the course of the Senegal-Mali negotiations of 1963–64.

Large waves of arrests are at least as common in the Ivory Coast as in Ghana, but they are not made public; the number of individuals under detention can only be estimated from the occasional announcement that a number of people have been released in celebration of a national holiday, Christmas, or another appropriate occasion. If coercion can be evaluated in terms of the total number of death sentences imposed by a government on its opponents, the Ivory Coast is probably the harshest country in Africa. Within a few days, at the beginning of 1963, the government obtained passage by the National Assembly of a law creating a special tribunal. Immediately afterwards a trap was set for alleged plotters against the security of the state and the President's life, and probably several hundred individuals were arrested. In April of that year, 86 of them were indicted and tried before the tribunal sitting behind closed doors in the President's own house, with the Secretary-General of the PDCI as prosecutor and other party officials composing the bench. Out of the total, 22 were acquitted; a number received small sentences ranging from 5 to 20 years; 7 were sentenced to imprisonment and hard labor for life; and 13 received the death penalty.

A few months later, many more persons, including several of the high party officials who had served on the April tribunal, were themselves accused of participating in a continuation of the orginal plot, arrested, and held for over a year without trial. In the spring of 1964 it was announced that one of them, a young French-trained lawyer who had been Minister of Education and then President of the Supreme Court, had committed suicide while under detention after confessing to particularly heinous crimes, including an attempt on the life of the President by means of voodoo techniques.[17] Shortly before the end of 1964, 19 acquittals, 19 jail sentences, 2 life sentences, and 6 death penalties were announced, without specifying who got what. Furthermore, 18 individuals who had been prominent in the party had

---

[17] A remarkable account of this event in the President's own words was published in *Abidjan-Matin,* April 16, 1964.

been found guilty but, because of services rendered, had been "absolved" on condition that they travel throughout the country and confess their crimes at mass rallies held for this purpose. Here also, it is necessary to stress that according to fairly reliable informants, none of the death sentences had been carried out at the time of writing.

THE INFLATIONARY SPIRAL OF COERCION AND VIOLENCE

From the preceding it is clear that the interaction between ruling groups and their opponents has produced a distinctive shift from one form of political conflict, which consisted mainly of electoral competition, social pressure to conform, and attempts by the dominant party to co-opt opponents, to another form of political conflict marked on the government side by more ruthless attempts to eliminate opponents by means of legal and extra-legal coercion, and on the other side by an increasing resort to violence, including civil disobedience and even political terrorism and assassination.

Two sets of qualifications are in order before this proposition can be properly understood.

(1) The earlier process of co-optation, negotiation, and reconciliation has never been fully superseded. What makes its survival possible is in part the fact that many opponents, whatever they may say while they are in opposition, fundamentally share the concern of the incumbents with political unity and are usually willing to participate in the ruling group when they have an opportunity to do so because in the small countries of West Africa, political office remains the single most important source of status and economic welfare. Two leading opposition politicians were included in the Guinean cabinet immediately after independence; in the Ivory Coast, a labor leader who was jailed for leading a strike that was declared illegal in 1959 turned up as a member of the National Assembly the following year; in Senegal two leaders of a small party were brought into the government as the result of a merger with the UPS as late as 1963; and although Ghana did not include any of the remaining opposition M.P.'s in the 1965 Parliament, several other former enemies became CPP representatives. In Ghana as elsewhere, one-party elections are used as a flexible device for political recruitment: the ruling group has control over the process in the sense that the results are never left to chance and that it retains the final word on approval of candidates, but the composition of the

final slate is arrived at through multiple compromises between local factions, between local groups and the central authorities, and probably between factions at the very top as well, in a manner that is unfortunately not readily observable by scholars.[18]

(2) When the details of the process are examined, analogies from European totalitarian states unavoidably come to mind even when the author makes no explicit attempt to suggest them. We think of them because African leaders themselves often use words we consider to be part of the jargon of totalitarian states to describe what they are doing. Sometimes this is completely fortuitous. Thus, when it is announced that a decision has been taken by the *Bureau Politique* of a French-speaking West African country, we are reminded of the Soviet Politburo, often forgetting that the Politburo term itself is derived from the original French and that *Bureau Politique* in the French tradition of leftist parties is the ordinary equivalent of the Anglo-American National Executive. In many cases, the borrowings are much more conscious, as with the phrases "democratic centralism," "internal contradictions," "mobilization," "deviations," or "anti-national opposition." The recurrent use of such terms almost inevitably leads observers to infer that their empirical referents in Africa must be identical with or at least very similar to their empirical referents in the Soviet Union or elsewhere. That this is a serious mistake, which even Soviet officials concerned with Africa have often made, becomes obvious when we try to reverse the example. All American students of comparative politics are taught very early that political terms such as "constitution," "federalism," "parliament," "supreme court," and especially "democracy," which are often used in other countries, usually do *not* refer to institutions or processes like the familiar American ones which they evoke. Whether or not African regimes are or are becoming totalitarian is of course a very important question which must be subjected to serious scrutiny; initially, however, we must reject the assumption that African systems necessarily resemble those from which they have borrowed much of their political discourse.

It is not only observers who are prone to make this mistake; strange as it may seem, West African political leaders themselves sometimes are caught up in the language they use. There is a sense in which they are "actors" in a more literal meaning than the one commonly used in social science literature. In the preceding chapter, it was

---
[18] See, however, the excellent analysis of the 1965 elections by J. M. Kraus in *Africa Report*, X, No. 8 (August, 1965), 6–11.

suggested that the creation of ideology was a ritual act. It can also be said that the political drama in which they are the leading actors is a ritual in the sense in which drama was originally, and remains fundamentally a symbolic enactment of a selective reality. Although perhaps all politics shares this quality, the newness of the African stage makes the quality more obvious and creates a very important confusion between dramatic and more commonplace reality. With this borrowed language, African leaders have constructed a political drama in which they enact what they believe to be appropriate behavior for the leaders of sovereign "mobilizing" nations. For example, the old political quarrels which persist after independence are acted out as a titanic battle between the Nation and the Anti-National Enemy. Strong-arm methods were always used to settle these quarrels, but now the enemy is arrested and must be brought to Trial. The courtroom scene begins: the Accused have endangered the Nation; hence, they are Traitors. Classically, a Nation is justified in reserving for Traitors the highest penalty. The climax is reached. The Judge dons his black cap and announces a Death Sentence. The world awaits the final scene, when the Traitors will die. But wait! As if they had never read the play to the end during rehearsal, the actors suddenly stop and go into a huddle. The accused are not strangers; they are simply annoying opponents whom we wish out of the way; yet they and the audience must be taught a severe lesson. The entire situation is now very embarrassing and an appropriate ending must be written quickly. Finally the play resumes for the final act. The Judge makes a solemn speech. "Let all Good Men Beware! This is how the Powerful Nation deals with Traitors!" But suddenly the Magnanimous Leader steps onto the stage: "The Wicked deserve to die, but their life will be spared. Justice must be tempered with Mercy." Curtain.

This is of course not a completely imaginary example, but constitutes what I believe to be a reasonable interpretation of what happened in Ghana and in the Ivory Coast, among others, in 1962–64. In this sort of situation, however, one is never sure whether the next time around the actors will return to reality in time or not; hence reality can become very like the play itself, with real men suffering real consequences.

Meanwhile, however, we must avoid taking the "totalitarian" play literally in all cases. Furthermore, the action is usually more complex than the one described above and the actors' potential is limited. The distinction between politics on and off the stage is important because it has been stated that the political process of new nations is characterized, among other things, by the fact that their leaders have a "high degree of freedom in determining matters of strategy and tactics."[19] In the light of the analysis above this generalization can be modified to suggest that although the leaders do have more autonomy than the leaders of other regimes in writing and enacting the play of their choice with little regard for the preferences of the critics or the wishes of the audience, it may be extremely difficult for them to effect a parallel transformation of society off-stage. This will become obvious in the next chapter when we consider attempts to create a new order. It may well be that because the gap between intentions and reality is much greater in African nations than in many other countries, politics takes on the character of drama in the hope that somehow the ritual of the play will have an effect on reality.

The fact that opponents have been eliminated with relative ease should not give us an exaggerated notion of the over-all power of the regimes. Unlike European totalitarians, Africans have had to destroy relatively little in the process of achieving a political monopoly. Although they have encountered some irritating obstacles, on the whole their task has been relatively easy because they did not have to subvert a generalized public conscience into acquiescence: none had yet been brought into being. It was seldom necessary to destroy democratic institutions: there were very few and even those were, after all, of very recent vintage and the heritage of foreign rule. In both spheres, the rulers moved into virgin territory; there they could plant symbols of their own choosing and begin the construction of a suitable political edifice. Plowing of the new ground was facilitated because in addition to the dominant party they had at their disposal the entire administrative and coercive apparatus inherited from the colonial power.

This helps explain why in spite of the growth of coercion, certain things have *not* happened. On the whole, repression has not been methodical and systematic. It has continued to take the form of attacks on specific individuals who are, from the point of view of the regime, dangerous or merely bothersome. Nowhere does the observer encounter a tendency to eliminate *categories* of individuals who are defined as enemies by virtue of an ascriptive characteristic, such as race or religion, or by virtue of their position in the economy, such as large landowners. From the point of view of an individual who is in jail for

---

[19]Pye, p. 659.

political reasons, it unfortunately matters little whether he is there as the result of a totalitarian trend or simply because someone decided that he must be kept out of the way for a while. But this makes a great difference from the point of view of our own understanding of the over-all regime and reminds us that it would be premature to conclude that the West African party-states have much in common with European totalitarianism.

With these two qualifications in mind, we can now return to the proposition stated at the beginning of this section. Acting in accordance with an ideological map which defines opposition as illegitimate, the ruling group attempts not only to neutralize and control visible political opponents, but furthermore to anticipate possible manifestations of opposition by establishing new electoral rules and coercive measures. Deprived of most legal channels for expressing discontent, various groups in the society engage in illegal action; the more dangerous this becomes, the more desperate their attempts to change the situation. This involves not only changing a team of rulers, but because the rulers are so closely identified with the political order, the entire regime.

The most evident manifestation of the trend has been a rash of plots. Although the validity of particular charges made by governments against their opponents is often questionable, these plots cannot be dismissed as figments of the leaders' imaginations. Although we can accept their existence, it is much more difficult to understand their structure. One of the remarkable aspects of plots in West Africa is that there seems to be a great deal of interchangeability of alliances among the disparate elements that oppose a particular regime. Thus, the leader of a plot which the government of Guinea described as "left-wing Marxist-Leninist" in late 1961, and which allegedly involved the Soviet Embassy, was led by a man who had organized an ethnic federation which opposed the PDG in 1954. Factionalism in Ghana since 1959 has been described alternatively as "right-wing" and "left-wing," but it is striking that many of the individuals allegedly involved tend to belong, regardless of their ideological orientation, to the Ga and Ewe peoples, who for various reasons have long opposed what they regard as Akan domination of Ghanaian politics. The Ivory Coast officially attributed all the strains of 1962–63 to a single plot, but its components appear to have been extremely heterogeneous: revolutionary-minded ex-students, old ethnic opponents, some French businessmen, and leaders of antagonistic factions within the PDCI. Asked to explain how such groups, which are known to have opposed one another earlier, had suddenly merged into a single illegal organization, a high party official threw up his hands and told his incredulous interviewer that he too could not believe it until he discovered the single thread that linked them all up: freemasonry.[20] A more reasonable way of accounting for such plots is to suggest that links among its components are usually very tenuous but that they are magnified beyond reality by the cabalistic cast of thought that prevails among the incumbents and by their need to justify strong measures, much as we saw in Chapter I was the case with colonial officials faced with nationalist agitation a decade earlier.

Paradoxically, it is the very success of the dominant parties in achieving political unanimity which has contributed most to growing insecurity in recent years. The co-optation of various elements into the ruling organization has not necessarily erased the differentiations that sustained opposing groups in the first place. Furthermore, the rewards of power have become so great that there is increasing competition among even the most faithful of lieutenants for the uppermost positions. As the state apparatus grows, differentiations among bureaucracies and among various types of services with competing clients tend to grow as well. How this has come about and how the regimes have attempted to cope with consequent problems will constitute the major themes of the next chapter. But it is already evident that the most important change in recent years has been the shift of opposition from outside the ruling organization to inside. There, opposition is even more frightening because it hides beneath a friendly guise; it is more threatening because it dwells very close to the center of power; it is more bewildering because it is no longer possible to know with assurance who is reliable and loyal. This shift reveals to the leaders in the cruelest way that all of their efforts to achieve unity in the only way they know are of little avail. The ideological map is ultimately a poor guide. Hence, an ever-increasing display of authority is necessary to obtain minimal reassurance that things will not fall apart.

---

[20]Interview with Philippe Yacé, Secretary-General of the PDCI and President of the National Assembly of the Ivory Coast (June, 1964).

CHAPTER IV

THE CREATION OF
A NEW INSTITUTIONAL ORDER

ALTHOUGH THE ELIMINATION OF OPPOSITION IN ITS VARIOUS FORMS IS SEEN by African leaders as a fundamental prerequisite for the achievement of unity or oneness, this is in a sense but a negative aspect, which consists of preventing certain undesirable political events. The activities entailed and the effort required are very different on the positive side, usually called in West Africa "the construction of the nation," which corresponds broadly to the concept "political integration" in the literature of the social sciences.[1] This requires the creation of effective political instruments which can be used by the rulers to bring about desired goals in every other domain. In all the countries considered, therefore, a very high priority has been assigned to the adaptation of the two major organizations, party and government, to the performance of new tasks defined by the one-party ideology. The relationship between these two instruments with different origins, traditions, and modes of organization is extremely difficult to define not only from the point of view of students of politics but from the vantage point of political practitioners as well. Following once again the procedure of earlier chapters, we shall consider each in turn, remembering that they constantly interact, and then conclude with a discussion of the interaction itself and of its consequences.

THE PARTY

It is naturally to the party that the rulers everywhere have assigned the performance of major tasks which they hope will lead to political

---

[1] For an explanation of this concept, see Myron Weiner, "Political Integration and Political Development," *Annals of the American Academy of Political and Social Science*, 358 (March, 1965), 52–64.

integration. They involve supervision, control, and co-ordination of all the other instruments of government; supplying individual and communal incentives for development; training both adults and children for citizenship in the new nation; serving as the concrete expression of that nation; acting as the major channel of communication between the leaders and the population and between the center and the localities, both downward by instructing the population concerning decisions, programs, and tasks, and upward in securing for the leaders necessary information and support.

The burdens that the party as an organization must shoulder are very heavy, not only because they include many tasks which in other societies are performed by other political agencies (e.g., as when the downward communication of government decisions is assured by existing mass media or when the family can be counted on to instill appropriate political values among new generations), but also because the new states were born very suddenly and everything must be done all at once. But how adequate were the dominant parties, as they emerged from the nationalist phase, for the performance of these manifold tasks? Their organization, their personnel, and the prevailing norms—the latent ideology of intermediate leaders and followers, in contrast to the forensic ideology of top leaders discussed in Chapter II—left a great deal to be desired because the parties had been fashioned by their experience as movements for the channeling of grievances and then as political machines admirably designed for the distribution of tangible rewards to leaders and followers. When instead it became necessary for the parties to act upon the society in accordance with the new goals, fundamental changes were clearly needed.

Serious attempts were made everywhere to bring this about. But everywhere it also quickly became apparent that many of the individuals who functioned successfully during the earlier period were not qualified by training or personality to carry out the new tasks; that it is difficult to devise multipurpose organizational mechanisms; and most crucially, that it is almost impossible for the party to remain an all-encompassing open membership group while at the same time becoming a reliable instrument of government. African leaders who speak a Marxist language have analyzed these problems in terms of internal "contradictions"; but whether they do so in precisely these terms or not, all have expressed their dismay at the gap between what the party is and what it ought to be, and the attempts to resolve these "contradictions" have taken strikingly similar forms in most countries.

THE CREATION OF A NEW INSTITUTIONAL ORDER

GHANA

Shortly after independence, President Kwame Nkrumah openly stressed the CPP's deficiencies in the face of the country's increasing needs and stated that the party must acquire a new organization and eliminate corruption among its personnel. A few years later he pointed out in retrospect that "when we met in 1958 in Koforidua, the national headquarters of the Party Secretariat was accommodated in a small office in Kimberley Avenue in Accra. The general staff numbered less than thirty. The office was poorly equipped and the administration was a sort of stop-gap arrangement."[2] In his Tenth Anniversary Speech of 1959, he again urged a reorganization because the party had become too heterogeneous and hence vulnerable to invasion by "petit bourgeois elements."[3] This would entail constructing a "grand alliance" with the trade unions and the farmers; the rebuilding of local branches into more disciplined bodies; extension of the party to reach the most remote village; the purge of "reactionary elements"; tightening of discipline on the basis of "democratic centralism"; and the creation of an inner core of "vanguard activists" properly trained in an ideological school.

Some of the elements of this program had already been launched. Shortly after independence, the party had appealed for half a million pounds to build a new headquarters in Accra and had announced the creation of an ideological wing, the National Association of Socialist Students' Organization (NASSO). But the major push came after the Tenth Anniversary Speech. By the end of 1959, the incumbent Secretary-General had been kicked upstairs, becoming Ambassador to Israel, and replaced by the organizer of NASSO, Tawia Adamafio. It was also announced that regional and district committees now existed everywhere and that their leaders were empowered to supervise administration. The status of party officials was visibly reinforced when regional commissioners were given ministerial rank and the secretary-general was given the title of ambassador. The party launched a youth movement and began to transform major voluntary associations such as trade unions and farmers' cooperatives into "party wings." An ideological institute was founded at Winneba, with the "Nassoists" as "vanguard activists."[4]

[2]*West Africa,* August 4, 1962.
[3]This and the following quotes are from *Speech Delivered by the Life Chairman on the Occasion of the Tenth Anniversary 12th June 1959 of the Convention People's Party* (Accra, no date).
[4]Details of party structure and regulations are contained in *The Constitution of the Convention People's Party* (revised) (Accra: Guinea Press, 1959).

95

The difficulties encountered by the party in implementing major items of this program can be guessed at from the important "Dawn" speech of May, 1961, when President Nkrumah denounced selfishness and profit-making by government and party officials, took personal control of the executive direction of the party, and announced that affiliation of labor unions and cooperatives to the party would no longer be indirect but direct. Shortly afterwards, the party press, now manned by new NASSO-type men, began a series of attacks on old-timers, including several party founders, on the grounds of inefficiency and corruption. Many of them resigned. It was then announced that functional or "place-of-work" branches would be created in all economic enterprises and in the midst of all social and cultural organizations; that the youth movement would be expanded and strengthened; and that party vigilante groups—named "Asafo companies" after young warriors' groups in traditional Akan society—would be created as party auxiliaries everywhere. Significantly, although this new wave of activity might have been taken as an indication of the fundamental transformation of the party into a genuinely elitist cadre organization, such an impression is incompatible with Nkrumah's subsequent criticism of party officials who obstruct admission or extort money from former opponents who want to join: "We cannot talk loudly of building a one-party state and yet drive away persons who would want to join the party and help to realize that objective." And in 1962 it was announced that the party had 2.5 million members (the bulk of the adult population) plus half a million youth-wingers of all ages.

How successful this new wave of reform was can be seen in the light of subsequent events: in spite of all efforts to transform the trade unions into a party wing, several of them struck against the government in late 1961; and the following year the trail followed by an investigation of the attempts on President Nkrumah's life led to Tawia Adamafio and H. Coffie-Crabbe, two leading architects of the 1959–62 party reorganization. Within a few months many of the old-timers dismissed a year earlier, such as Krobo Edusei, N. A. Welbeck, and Kojo Botsio, were reinstated. The President once more took the lead in criticizing the CPP, followed obediently by many officials. Among the items mentioned during a series of seminars, the following reveal the state of the party: "Party solidarity needs strengthening and the sense of oneness among the M.P.'s, the T.U.C. [Trades Union Congress, a party wing], or Farmers Council officials [another wing], or District Commissioner, Regional Commissioner [the party administrators referred to above] and/or Regional Secretary founded on membership of the Party is practically non-existent"; "Communication between the Party Organization and its members is not in keeping with the Party's progressive directives"; field officials view their jobs as the issuing of directives from their office, forgetting that "the bigger part is to go out into the field and see that the Party programme is carried out to the letter, with the full support and enthusiasm of the people."[5]

In the by then familiar way, the party began to transform itself once more, following the model of a "mobilizing" organization. In a direct reversal of the President's statement of a year earlier enjoining officials to admit everyone, the party seminar stated that "recent events have clearly shown that the Party solidarity has been gravely undermined by putting into effect this directive and the chaos that followed is now a common place."[6] New rules prevented anyone from holding party or public office unless he had served in the party for five years, except by special dispensation of the Central Committee. Furthermore, an ethnic association (Ga) which had existed *within* the party was disbanded; citizenship training in the schools was stepped up and all pupils were required to wear "Young Pioneer" uniforms; Winneba began to dispense a two-year ideological diploma course; and N. A. Welbeck announced a "purge" of Adamafio and Crabbe followers. But the implications of other decisions are much less clear: henceforth, M.P.'s, who hitherto seemed to have been overshadowed by administrative officials, had to be consulted in the nomination of district commissioners and their role to be considered as "supervisory"; in order to clarify party communications and stamp out rumors, the party recommended the creation of local committees which, surprisingly, could "consist of a Magistrate, a Paramount Chief, and any independent third person."

In recent years, the CPP has continued on the same idiosyncratic course: political district commissioners have come under fire because of widespread corruption, and a commission headed by an Englishman was appointed in mid-1964 to investigate and check all irregularities, misconduct, and malpractices among CPP and state officials. Following the discovery that the TUC national secretary was disloyal, a new official was appointed, but he resigned a month later because of financial irregularities; for years the CPP had stressed ideological education,

---

[5]*Towards Socialism* (Accra: Government Printer, 1962), p. 12.
[6]*Ibid.*, p. 19.

but it was only when a visiting British Communist expressed surprise at finding that the contents of libraries and bookshops in Ghana were much like those in Britain that the party created a committee to inspect bookshops and libraries in order to remove all "anti-CPP" publications; the stress on political socialization of youth began in 1957, but it was only at the end of 1964 that the CPP established a branch at the University of Ghana.

What is the CPP like a decade and a half after its founding and nearly ten years after independence? Not even the most experienced observers have been able to provide a satisfactory answer to this question. Visiting Ghana shortly after the referendum of 1964 on the one-party state amendment, one of them commented:

> . . . few people in Ghana, and fewer still outside, have any clear idea of how the party is organized, how it is financed, how its leaders are chosen, how its policies are formulated, how its functionaries are appointed or dismissed. Even the names of some of those most influential in its councils are not well known.[7]

After a year in the field, a student of Ghanaian politics had not been able to obtain a complete roster of the ruling committees of the party, less because this was considered to be secret information than because nobody in Ghana seemed to know or even to think that such knowledge was very important; his general impression was that the omnipresent CPP was in reality very hard to find.[8]

What is the CPP? President Nkrumah told the world several years ago: The CPP is Ghana. It has almost ceased to be a tangible separate organization; far from transforming Ghana into its own image, it has come to reflect all the cleavages, components, norms, and structures that prevail in an underdeveloped country. But while it is difficult to know with any certainty *what the CPP is,* we should have from the preceding a very good idea of *what it is not.* Given the present state of our understanding of West African politics, this constitutes definite progress.

---

[7]"Matchet," in *West Africa,* February 8, 1964.
[8]These impressions are derived from innumerable conversations with Ernst Benjamin, now at Wayne State University, whose interesting work on Ghanaian politics is in process. This helps explain how easily the Army could carry out a coup in 1966 and the apparent lack of reaction to its subsequent decision to "disband" the CPP.

IVORY COAST

Somewhat paradoxically, in the light of the antagonism that has prevailed between the leaders of the Ivory Coast and Ghana during the past decade and their sharply different stands on a variety of economic and international issues, the general impression obtained from an examination of the CPP is replicated when we look at the PDCI. In spite of its overwhelming success as a vote-getting organization, the PDCI acknowledged its inadequacies when the first congress in ten years was held in 1959. The *Bureau Politique* criticized itself and was criticized by others for having neglected organization, imposed sloppy controls on party finances, lacked initiative, and ignored internal democracy.[9] The congress produced a reformed party, with the first properly elected *Bureau Politique* and *Comité Directeur* since 1949, which reflected the changing composition of the party by including, besides old-timers, officials of a newly created youth wing (JRDACI), trade unionists, prominent women, as well as leaders of several ex-opposition groups. It was headed by a new Secretary-General, Jean-Baptiste Mockey, generally thought to be a forceful man and somewhat independent of the President's authority. Shortly afterwards, the party launched a weekly newspaper, affirming its resolution to modernize itself by eliminating the ethnic committees which composed its branches in major towns, and announced a new membership drive with stress on the payment of annual dues.[10]

By the end of 1959 there were indeed many indications of a revival of party activity, with teams of organizers traveling throughout the country to revive some branches and to create new ones, as well as to organize the JRDACI. There was a slight interruption when Mockey was deposed, probably because of disagreement with the President on the then-current issue of independence. The new Secretary-General, Philippe Yacé, a man known to be more subservient to the President, announced that the PDCI was "a dying political party," proceeded to purge Mockey followers, and resumed the implementation of congress decisions. In 1961–62, the party program was extended to include the creation of special branches for civil servants who had hitherto resisted

---

[9] The Ivory Coast material up to 1961 is drawn from the author's *One-Party Government in the Ivory Coast* (Princeton: Princeton University Press, 1964).

[10] The case of the party organization is discussed in detail in the author's "Mass Parties and National Integration: The Case of the Ivory Coast," *Journal of Politics*, XXV, No. 1 (February, 1963), 36–48.

attempts to form a government-controlled union; a campaign to raise 150 million CFA francs to build a new party headquarters; the establishment of political commissions in each ministry; and ideological rededication in the form of party seminars such as the one cited in Chapter II.

As in Ghana, there were many difficulties. First, the youth wing, thought to have become too autonomous, was disbanded at the national level and local committees were brought under the direct supervision of officials of the senior party; then, the internal reorganization of the PDCI by elimination of its ethnic components was abandoned because "men are slower than ideas."[11] Following the first "plot" of 1963, nearly half of the former national executive of the youth wing and an unknown number of lesser figures in the PDCI, the JRDACI, and other affiliated organizations were detained; in September, 1963, it was the turn of several senior members of the PDCI's *Bureau Politique,* many political administrators, and several former opponents. To what extent the party was disrupted during this period can be gauged from the fact that its congress, first announced for 1962, was postponed repeatedly.

Following these severe crises, a new attempt was made to forge an effective and loyal party apparatus. During the remainder of 1963 and 1964 the trade-union organization was unified under the leadership of politically reliable men; a national women's wing was organized; party militias, distinct from the regular police and the army, were constituted; and the party newspaper became a daily. Following a reorganization of the political administration of the country, thirty-six additional PDCI branches were created to correspond to the new *sous-préfectures;* this as well as the revival of numerous other branches was accomplished under the supervision of roving teams composed of the remaining members of the *Bureau Politique* and other politicians, and unusual publicity was given to elections of branch officials in the party press.

Having surmounted these crises, the party leadership finally felt sufficiently confident to hold its first congress since independence on September 23–25, 1965. The official mood was summarized by the inscription on the giant banner which dominated the stage of the newly completed, air-conditioned party headquarters in Treichville: "A single party, for a single people, with a single leader." Clearly the most significant aspect of the Congress was that it constituted a serious attempt

---

[11]*Ibid.;* there had been no change as of mid-1964.

to restore the party to its place of eminence in the country, as if to give the lie to those who had been speaking of its decline. The *Bureau Politique* and the *Comité Directeur,* whose membership had been depleted as the result of the recurrent internal crises since 1959, were enlarged by the addition of a number of women, a sprinkling of university graduates, but most strikingly by the promotion of many "old militants" whose names were closely associated with the glorious period 1948-51. Furthermore, for the first time, the Secretaries-General of party branches became paid officials, with salaries ranging from $200 to $400 a month; they, together with leaders of affiliated trade unions, women's and students' organizations, will constitute the National Committee. The party's plan to launch "JET," a new national movement for young people aged fourteen to twenty-five, was also announced. Although it was rumored that there had been an internal contest for party leadership, this never reached the surface and Philippe Yacé became once again Secretary-General of the PDCI.[12]

GUINEA[13]

If in the Ivory Coast, and to a lesser extent in Ghana, it is difficult to discern the party as a separate instrument within the general organization of government, there is no doubt at all about the visibility of the party in Guinea, and especially in Mali. While at independence Ghana was left with a well-trained indigenous civil service and the Ivory Coast and Senegal continued to rely for their administration on numerous French officials, Guinea and Mali became independent under tense circumstances and hence were thrown rather abruptly on their own. Neither country had much of a civil service; hence, the party emerged by default as almost the sole instrument of rule. It is not surprising, therefore, to find that the party became responsible for many services normally considered to be within the sphere of administration.

---

[12]For reports of the Congress, see *Fraternité,* issues of September 24, October 1, and October 8, 1965; *West Africa,* October 2; *Jeune Afrique* (September 30–October 6).

[13]I shall not discuss the case of Senegal in detail because I have not been able to acquire sufficient information to make such a discussion worthwhile. The Senegalese case appears to resemble that of the Ivory Coast, with the government playing an increasingly important role. There is more openness in the party, however, as indicated by the relative regularity of party congresses. The problem of internal factionalism came to a head in the conflict between "Senghorists" and "Diaists" in 1962 and was followed by a purge of "Diaists" from the party. For Senegal to 1962, see the excellent chapter by William Foltz in James S. Coleman and Carl G. Rosberg, Jr., *Political Parties and National Integration in Tropical Africa* (Berkeley and Los Angeles: University of California Press, 1964), pp. 16–64.

Because both countries are prone to express themselves in Marxist language, much of what happened was described as the establishment, Soviet-style, of a party administration parallel to government bureaucracies. In reality, however, it was more a matter of making ends meet with relatively inexperienced personnel, usually low-level civil servants who had shortly before been appointed to second European administrators in preparation for independence, and who had been promoted on the basis of the only reasonable alternative criterion, political reliability.

The PDG came to power with ancillary bodies that were perhaps more important than the party itself. Before 1957 it consisted primarily of a strong trade-union wing and a powerful women's organization, with a relatively recent and weak network of constituency branches. It was only after it controlled the government of Guinea that the party began to affirm its territorial organization. Immediately after independence, this expansion was accelerated. Official announcements claimed that the number of party cards issued doubled between 1959 and 1961, reaching 1.6 million (almost complete saturation of the adult population) in the latter year; one observer reported that there were about 4,000 basic party committees in 1961[14]; and President Sékou Touré referred to 7,164 of them, plus women's and youth committees, the following year. Originally they had been organized into forty-three *sections* corresponding to administrative districts (*subdivisions*); by 1961 the number of *sections* had grown to 163, apparently the result of splitting them up into smaller units to correspond to the newly created administrative posts. Although information about this period is difficult to come by, it is likely that in most localities these party units represented the only tangible link with the center.[15] The PDG also obtained a monopoly over written communications when the only daily newspaper, part of a French-owned chain, ceased its operations in Conakry.

The PDG has experienced the usual difficulties encountered by governmental parties in West Africa. After a number of officials of the youth wing were allegedly involved in a "left-wing" plot in 1961, there was evidence of much activity involving the renewal of branch officials

---

[14] Victor DuBois, "The Independence Movement in Guinea: A Study in African Nationalism," (Unpublished dissertation, Princeton University, Department of Political Science, 1962), p. 321. See also his article in Coleman and Rosberg, pp. 186–215.

[15] In addition to DuBois, see L. Gray Cowan, "Guinea," in Gwendolen M. Carter (ed.), *African One-Party States* (Ithaca: Cornell University Press, 1962), pp. 149–245; and Bernard Charles, "Un Parti politique africain: le Parti Démocratique de Guinée," *Revue Française de Science Politique,* XII, No. 2 (June, 1962), 312–59. The latter contains in particular a remarkable amount of quantitative information.

throughout the country; like the CPP in Ghana, the PDG announced that henceforth party officials at the lowest and intermediate levels must have three and five years of service respectively before appointment or election. Government officials were no longer eligible for office in party branches, but they were made *ex officio* members—perhaps a way of insuring that even unpopular officials find a secure place within party councils at the local level. In keeping with the general trend toward reduction of consultation within the party, it was decided at the sixth PDG congress, held in December, 1962, that this assembly would henceforth take place every five years rather than every three; but the following year the *Bureau Politique* suddenly constituted itself into a congress, eliminated two members from its own midst, and dissolved the committees they had headed, which suggests the persistence of factionalism.

In 1963 the party was reformed to parallel a new administrative reorganization which stressed decentralization. The old basic committees remained; the *sections* seemed to have been split into even smaller units which grew to a total of 1,652; above them were constituted new federations to correspond to the thirty regions into which the country had been divided under the reorganization. The following year it was announced that the youth and women's committees were being disbanded, the usual clue that they had been growing into autonomous organizations. Furthermore, party authorities then decided that decentralization had gone too far; in Conakry, for example, the number of basic PDG committees had grown from 60 to 173. In commenting on this, President Sékou Touré provided a rare glimpse into the true nature of the party: he stated that "certain committees did not represent more than two or three families and the membership was dominated by family discipline or by the family chief who was at the same time the president of the committee."[16] In a society where for many of the ethnic groups kinship and political structure coincided, this indicated that after six years of intensive effort, the party, far from transforming society, had come to reflect its persisting traditional features.

MALI

During the difficult period following the break-up of the Federation of Senegal and Sudan, when their country's very survival was at

---

[16] Quoted in *Afrique Nouvelle*, November 20, 1964.

stake and the economy almost came to a standstill, the leaders of the *Union Soudanaise* appealed to the population of the capital to contribute their labor and scarce resources to the construction of a new party headquarters. *La Maison du Parti,* built in 1960, is a tangible symbol of the prominence of the party in the political life of Mali. As in Guinea, so in Mali the effort to transform the nationalist movement into a powerful instrument of government began immediately after the leaders of the *Union Soudanaise* came to power under the *Loi-Cadre* decrees of 1957. There was much to be done, as the Prime Minister and Secretary-General, Modibo Keita told the assembled party congress in 1958. Complaining that in the wake of the March, 1957, victory, the party had become "demobilized," he reminded them that "the dynamism of the political and economic action of an organization is a function of the quality of its organization."[17] He proposed, with the approval of the congress, that the party extend its activities into all the villages, wards, offices, and factories; that the newspaper be printed instead of mimeographed; and that ancillary bodies be reinforced. After the congress it was also decided to extend party control rapidly over the territorial administration by replacing expatriate political officials with Africans. There is little doubt among Malians that it was this effort which enabled the country to survive politically during the crisis of 1960.

By the time the next full-scale party congress was held in 1962, the party claimed to have organized basic committees in every village, ward, office, factory, and even among the *fractions* into which the Sahara nomads are divided for administrative purposes. All these committees were said to have youth and women's affiliates which were organized into national wings, along with labor unions and veterans. Attached to many urban branches are also *brigades de vigilance,* usually a group of young men empowered to perform police duties, who spend most of their time stopping nocturnal pedestrian and vehicular traffic for a variety of purposes, which included, according to various informants, checks on smuggling, subversion, and on payment of party dues, as well as the enforcement of standards of sexual morality. A party inspectorate, consisting of roving commissioners responsible to the *Bureau Politique* and empowered to suspend and reorganize branches, was created in 1961. Although membership figures have never

---

[17]US-RDA, "Documents" (Bamako, 1959; mimeographed), p. 8; and *L'Essor,* August 16, 1958. For the general organization of the US during the period to 1962, see in particular the chapter by Thomas Hodgkin and Ruth Morgenthau in Coleman and Rosberg.

been published, an estimate based on representation at the 1962 congress suggests a figure of about half a million (one-fourth of all adults), approximately a tenfold increase over 1958.[18] By 1964, party dues seemed to be collected as a matter of course from all adults by government as well as party officials along with annual personal taxes.[19]

It is extremely difficult to discern trends in party organization since 1962. Following the congress, the national executive of the youth wing was disbanded because it had shown the usual tendency to act autonomously, and the local youth committees were placed under the direct control of local party branches. Although there were few changes in the *Bureau Politique,* several members, thought to represent the most revolutionary tendency, were not reappointed. Of great organizational significance was the fact that the old *Comité Directeur,* which consisted mostly of elected leaders of local branches, was eliminated and replaced by a *Conférence Nationale des Cadres,* which includes not only party officials but also government administrators and elected representatives who do not hold office in the party apparatus. That this might indicate a relative decline in the importance of the party as an organization at the expense of professional government bureaucrats (who are, as they are everywhere else, members of the party) is confirmed by the condemnation at the 1962 congress of a "deviation" in the interpretation of the concept of party supremacy: this means, it was explained, that the party formulates general policies which are then executed by the government; it does *not* mean that party officials at the district level have authority over government officials.[20]

In spite of these qualifications, there is no doubt that in Mali perhaps more than anywhere else, the party remains the most prominent political institution. What that means, however, must be understood in context. Although the party newspaper is the only one in the country, its daily circulation is only about 1,500 copies, and the larger weekly edition runs to about 3,000, of which perhaps half remain in the capital. The huge network of party organizations seems to devote most of its time and effort to the verbal communication of directives from the center, including routine announcements of the passage of new laws, of the negotiation of foreign treaties, or of public holidays, which otherwise might never reach the bulk of the population. How effec-

---

[18] My own computations, based on information contained in *VIe Congrès de l'USRDA* (Bamako: Editions Librairie Populaire, 1963). The Political Secretary of the party, when asked to comment, seemed to nod in approval of the estimate.
[19] Personal observations during the first half of 1964.
[20] *VIe Congrès . . .,* pp. 71–73.

tively the party has performed even this most basic task is questionable in the light of the need for a decision in late 1964 enjoining each party branch to appoint a permanent secretary who, in the absence of the secretary-general who is often an official residing in the capital, will be on the spot when the messages arrive.

THE GOVERNMENT

Speaking of Guinea, L. Gray Cowan pointed to the dominance of the party over government and concluded that "the source of political power is expressly kept outside the provisions of the constitution, and the subordination of all organs of government to the party organization render meaningless the constitutional relationships of these organs to one another."[21] Since this comment applies to other countries as well, it is evident that an examination of the formal institutions will not tell us much about how decisions are actually made or how power is distributed. That, however, is not our purpose in this section; we shall consider instead how the rulers of the West African states have used the institutional legacy they received at the time of independence in order to further our understanding of the political order they are trying to create. Because of this it is necessary once again to take into account the initial base line. In the political sphere more than in other spheres, there were important differences between terminal colonial arrangements in Ghana and in French-speaking West Africa.

We have already pointed out that Ghana began its independent life with a genuine civil service and with legal institutions manned by Ghanaian magistrates and sustained in their operations by a well-established corps of trained lawyers. Although the Ghanaian parliament was modeled after that at Westminster, it was in one major respect less sovereign than its counterpart: while in Great Britain there is no legal rule that cannot be changed by a simple act of Parliament, the Ghanaian constitution of 1957 contained "entrenched" clauses requiring two-thirds majorities for their modification. They pertained in particular to the protection of regional and local institutions of self-government within which traditional chiefs retained substantial authority. The powers of the Ghanaian Prime Minister were similar to those of his British counterpart; as in Britain, he was effective head of gov-

---

[21] L. Gray Cowan, in Carter, p. 208.

ernment, with the Queen—represented in Ghana by a Governor-General under the Statute of Westminster which rules arrangements for Commonwealth States—as head of state. This was a ceremonial office, to be sure, but it meant that the authority of the state continued to be symbolized on currency and elsewhere by the image of the colonial ruler. Thus, the Ghanaian system of government contained checks on majority rule which are much more in the American tradition than in the British; symbolically, African politicians shared authority with a British Queen; and also although Britain had rejected the federal arrangements sought by the opposition, Ghana was somewhat more decentralized than Britain itself and secular leaders also shared their authority with traditional leaders. This political decentralization was somewhat offset by the fact that Ghana retained the colonial system of field administrators representing the central authority (district officers, etc.), a device that resembles the continental system of prefects and is foreign to Anglo-Saxon administrative traditions.

The situation was quite different in French-speaking Africa where, from the very beginning, executive authority was broader than that of parliament. Until 1957, the domain over which African assemblies could make rules was restricted to local matters, with the French parliament alone retaining the right to legislate on many others. When the Fifth Republic was established as an executive-dominant system in which the legislative authority of parliament was specifically curtailed while executive authority to make rules was extended, the new African states followed suit. Political and administrative centralization were firmly established also. The chiefs had long been deprived of any autonomous authority and had become low-level agents of the central government; there was no tradition of effective regional councils; and municipal government had only recently begun to operate under the strict supervision of the central administration. Except to some extent in Senegal, Africanization of the upper ranks of the civil service had barely begun and there was therefore no indigenous bureaucracy with a tradition of apolitical service. The judiciary was manned almost entirely by European magistrates; there had not yet developed a substantial body of legal-minded Africans. Senegal alone differentiated between the offices of head of state and head of government, but even there both were manned by Africans from the outset. And although membership in the French Community—which only Senegal retained after independence—involved certain obligations, it did not involve the sharing of authority symbols that was found in Ghana.

From these different points of departure the five countries began to move toward a common focal point: a system of government with a monocephalic and nearly sovereign executive; a national assembly that is consultative rather than legislative and which is based on functional and corporate representation rather than geographical and individual; a centralized political administration that has been expanded to reach more minute local components and modified to be more exclusively secular; mechanisms of local government from which the "self" has been removed; and a governmental bureaucracy in which the criterion of political loyalty is given overwhelming weight.

THE NATIONAL EXECUTIVE

Whatever the particular arrangements laid down in West African constitutions, in all countries the President rules relatively unhampered either by a separation of powers or by other limiting definitions of his authority. The Ivory Coast was the first of the French-speaking countries to abandon completely the parliamentary system and to adopt a Presidential system whose mechanisms resemble the American: the chief executive, who is both head of state and head of government, is elected on the basis of universal suffrage and appoints a cabinet that is not accountable to the Assembly. But in both the constitution and in reality, Presidential authority is much broader: the legislature's authority is limited by enumerating the matters that are within its domain, while the residual power is the executive's; furthermore "Though the constitution gives the Assembly power to decide fundamental matters, Houphouet really makes these decisions."[22] Guinea had a President elected by the National Assembly and responsible to it, much like a Prime Minister, but who could appoint his own cabinet; this was modified in 1961 to a more purely Presidential system with the chief executive elected for a seven-year term by universal suffrage. Mali has retained formal arrangements much like those devised initially by Guinea.

For some time, Senegal remained the exception. Until the beginning of 1963, its formal arrangements for the executive resembled those which prevailed initially in the Fifth Republic, with an indirectly elected President-head of state and a Prime Minister-head of government responsible to the Assembly. This division of authority was re-

---

[22]A. S. Alexander, Jr., "The Ivory Coast Constitution," *Journal of Modern African Studies*, I, No. 3 (September, 1963), 308.

inforced by the fact that the men who filled it, while belonging to the same party, had relatively separate bases of political power. It is therefore significant that a latent conflict between them finally reached the point of explosion in late 1962, when there was a showdown between Prime Minister Mamadou Dia and President Senghor in which it is still extremely difficult to determine which of the two really staged a *coup d'état* against the other.[23] After President Senghor's victory, Senegal modified its constitution in the direction of the Ivory Coast model. In all these cases the chief executive can also quite easily obtain additional powers to rule by decree for specified periods when an emergency has been declared by the Assembly, which is, of course, usually subservient to his wishes.

The Ghanaian leadership began to express its desire to create a republic shortly after independence and finally proposed a constitutional amendment to this effect in 1959. The explanation for this move, in light of the popularity of the Queen of England throughout the country, provides an interesting clue to an understanding of the rulers' concerns: "When we talk about a Republic it is not because we do not like monarchs but because people feel that an independent African state like Ghana *should have a leader they can see*. If there is trouble, then the head will be with us, not thousands of miles away."[24] As we saw earlier, this amendment was approved by referendum in 1960, concurrently with the popular election of President Nkrumah. Four years later the system was modified to provide for Presidential elections by the single-party parliament acting as an electoral college, but the President retained the upper hand, since he has the right to dissolve the Assembly at any time, whereupon new elections must follow within two months. President Nkrumah was re-elected in this manner in June, 1965. As in the other cases, there has also been great broadening of the domain of executive authority in Ghana.

All five presidents are also effective heads of their respective parties even where there is a formal distinction between the offices of party President and party Secretary-General, as in the Ivory Coast. Since African leaders believe that the authority of the state must be personalized if it is to carry any weight, the monocephalic tendency is further reinforced by numerous informal and symbolic devices. Thus Nkrumah explained in 1957 when some objected to a decision to place his profile on a new issue of coinage: "because many of my people cannot read or write, they have to be shown that they are now really

[23] See the discussion appended to Foltz's chapter in Coleman and Rosberg.
[24] Quoted in *The Times* (London), January 3, 1959; my emphasis.

independent. And they can be shown only by signs."[25] The Maliens resorted to precisely the same device when they adopted their own currency in 1962; when asked whether the presence of President Modibo Keita's image on every single item of paper money was not incompatible with the stress on "collective leadership," officials resorted to an explanation which repeated almost word for word Nkrumah's statement.

The style in which this personalization of executive authority is expressed varies somewhat. Thus in Ghana, where the British monárchy has become almost as traditional as pre-European African culture, the title "President" is probably not very significant. It is therefore not surprising to find that Kwame Nkrumah has been honored with additional titles such as *Osagyefo,* an Akan term sometimes said to mean "redeemer" or "savior," but rendered more accurately by "victorious one" or the old Roman term, "Imperator." The inclusion of the Akan sacred stool among the paraphernalia of Presidential office suggests continuity with traditional African authority, and is perhaps an attempt to make up for the fact that Nkrumah doesn't belong to an eminent chiefly lineage. When the President is greeted at rallies with hymns such as "Lead, Kindly Light," we must remember that Protestantism is now also a major ingredient of Ghanaian culture. And if the political use of terms normally reserved for the deity appears shocking, we might do well to remember that the word "supreme," which hardly arouses attention when coupled with "court" in the United States, rang very differently when it was initially bestowed upon the English monarch during the sixteenth century in sharp opposition to the hitherto "supreme" power of Rome.

In contrast with Ghana, the title of "President" evokes respect throughout most French-speaking Africa. In Mali there is evidently little need to bestow on the President additional titles that have traditional connotations since even non-Malinké know that the Keitas are a ruling lineage, while in Guinea a Touré who claims descent from the Almamy Samory might be looked upon much as was a Bonaparte in mid-nineteenth-century France. Although there is some debate over President Houphouet-Boigny's personal status as a traditional leader, he is known to belong to a family of Baoulé chiefs; when the Baoulé paramount leader died a few years ago, no successor was chosen because it was suggested that Houphouet-Boigny implicitly filled that

---

[25] Quoted in *West Africa,* June 29, 1957.

office. Although in the Ivory Coast the President's image does not appear on the currency, which has not been changed since the colonial period, it has appeared on postage stamps and is visible in almost every house.

Everywhere in West Africa the presidency has been surrounded with conspicuous physical trappings. Honor guards abound and it is common to clear all traffic from the highway on which the President is traveling—a measure which has been criticized in Malawi, for example, but which is fully understandable to anyone who has traveled on the same unsafe roads. The presidents also live in sumptuous buildings. In Mali, Guinea, and Senegal, they have all moved into the former governors' palaces; President Nkrumah followed suit after some hesitation, and moved into Christianborg citadel, renamed Osu, arguing once again the need to make the shift of authority from Europeans to Africans clearly visible. President Houphouet-Boigny chose instead to raze the old governor's palace (after the Ivory Coast had spent a great deal to modernize it) and to erect on the same spot a glass, steel, and marble marvel which leaves no doubt as to where power lies.

Monocephalism may or may not coincide with the growth of absolute autocratic despotism. No African leader so far has exhibited the quality of madness associated with modern tyrants such as Hitler or Stalin; none rules without consultation or exclusively in accordance with his personal whims. Almost everywhere it is possible to identify trusted advisers and lieutenants, often co-founders of the party, regional strongmen, and technocrats—occasionally expatriates—who have relatively free access to the President and to whom he is known to listen. This is particularly true where the President was not the original founding father, as in Mali where in 1956 Modibo Keita was but one of several possible political heirs to the late Mamadou Konaté, and it may become a generalized feature of the West African party-state as the incumbents depart. Meanwhile, however, even in Mali, there is as little doubt as to who is the boss as there was when the country was ruled by a colonial governor.

NATIONAL ASSEMBLIES

The counterpart to the growth of executive dominance has been the downgrading of the legislative function of national conciliar organs. We must be careful in this respect, however, not to use the

American model as a standard of evaluation since the United States Congress is unique in the contemporary world as a representative body which retains important *legislative* functions; that is not the case in Great Britain, for example, because of the control of party majorities by the executive, nor in France under the Fifth Republic. At best, as in Great Britain, the national representative body functions as a debating chamber where the opposition can air its criticism of government policy but usually knows that little can be done to alter it before the next election. With the elimination of opposition in Africa, even this function is, of course, not being performed.

The executive has the final word. What is striking, however, is that these regimes do not find it desirable to maintain even the public façade of debate. Since it can be assumed that this could easily be arranged, we must conclude that the desire to demonstrate unanimity is greater than the concern to demonstrate the persistence of democracy. This helps explain why it is possible that beneath the surface, national assemblies actually *do* perform significant functions. Although formal debate disappeared from the National Assembly of Guinea as early as 1958, and in the Ivory Coast and Mali around 1959, there is evidence in both the Ivory Coast and Mali that at least some of the proposals submitted by the executive have occasionally been delayed or seriously modified by committees of the National Assembly and eventually passed unanimously only after some of these alterations had been taken into consideration. In Senegal, the National Assembly remained lively until the crisis of 1962-63, in which it played an important role. The parliamentary spirit has survived longest in Ghana, where even in the spring session of 1965, CPP backbenchers still openly challenged the government on such important matters as the program of state farms, and, it was estimated, about 400 questions were submitted to government during question periods.[26] In Ghana, more than elsewhere, the information without which such queries would be impossible is made available: the auditor-general's report on government finances is published every year and annual reports for most ministries can be procured from the Government Printer.

Although formally laws must be approved by the national assemblies provided for under the various constitutions, there seems to be a general trend toward the growth of another type of national council that is broader and more flexible. Much as the national organs of the

---

[26] I am grateful to Ron Bayer, graduate student at the University of Chicago, for bringing the state farms debate to my attention.

THE CREATION OF A NEW INSTITUTIONAL ORDER

party have come to include other components—especially wings and government officials—so members of parliament or *députés* have become but one set of representatives, alongside others such as party officials, etc. In some cases the constitution itself provides for institutions such as the *Conseil Economique et Social* of the Ivory Coast, with individuals nominated on the basis of economic representation; such institutions probably have at least as much influence on government economic policy as the National Assembly. Furthermore, the meetings called by President Houphouet-Boigny in January and September, 1963, constituted a sort of Estates-General of the Ivory Coast: they included members of the government; the *Bureau Politique;* the *Comité Directeur,* and secretaries-general of PDCI sections; members of the National Assembly and of regional councils; the Supreme Court; all Ivory Coast ambassadors; administrative heads of departments; the prefects plus six chiefs and twelve notabilities from each prefecture; two members of each ethnic committee in Abidjan; and finally representatives of women's organizations, youth groups, veterans, etc. In composition and in spirit this resembles very closely the *Conférence Nationale des Cadres* which is periodically assembled in Mali to listen to major policy announcements and possibly also discuss them. Parliaments themselves may take on this character: speaking of the one-party parliament that would be elected in Ghana, for example, President Nkrumah referred to a "corporate body" made up of farmers, workers, artisans, factory workers, teachers, managers, engineers, intellectuals and university professors, doctors, members of the civil service, members of public boards, and of the judiciary.[27]

With the elimination of political competition, recruitment to these bodies, albeit formally by election, is tantamount to appointment by the executive. But although the executive can always make sure that the men it wishes to include in it will be included and that the men it does not want included will not be, there is a large margin for bargaining between the central authorities and various groups and localities between these limits. Turnover has been fairly high: in Mali, for example, one-fourth of the National Assembly elected in 1964 consisted of new members; in Guinea, the bulk of the sixty elected in 1963 were also new; Ghana increased the total number of representatives in 1965 from 114 to 198; some of the incumbents were not re-elected, which

---

[27] Quoted in *West Africa*, February 8, 1964; early results of the 1965 elections seem to confirm this corporate trend, as suggested by Jon Kraus in *Africa Report*, X, No. 8 (August, 1965), 6–11.

indicates that about half of the members were new. Similarly, only 48 of 70 members of the Ivory Coast National Assembly originally elected in 1960 were re-elected in November, 1965; in the new assembly, enlarged to 85, 37 were newcomers.

On the whole, then, with evidence of relatively flexible recruitment and changing membership, we can conclude that national assemblies and the new corporate councils continue to be genuinely representative. They are not democratic parliaments, but important consultative bodies which provide, after the executive machinery and the party, a third major means of communication between the rulers and the population. Beneath a modern parliamentary guise, they resemble closely in composition and function the early legislative councils or *conseils généraux* of the colonial system as well as European parliaments before they were fully democratized.

REGIONAL AND LOCAL GOVERNMENT

The West African states have on the whole retained the general system of "field" or "political" administration established by the colonial rulers but have increased the over-all density of government, so to speak, by providing more direct contact between this administration and the population. The traditional component in this administrative grid has been reduced or totally eliminated, at least formally. The fate of regional, rural, and urban representative councils has closely paralleled that of national assemblies.

The typical arrangement for territorial political administration in French Africa included at the top a governor; below a *commandant* who ruled over the *cercle;* then a (European) *chef de subdivision;* beneath these, a large number of *cantons* to which the administration appointed an African chief with or without traditional legitimacy; and finally (in the rural areas) a village chief or headman who normally did have the right to rule according to custom. Since independence the trend has been to create between the center and the old *cercle* a new level of administration usually called a department or region; the old subdivisions have been renamed *cercle* or *sous-préfecture;* the *canton* has usually been eliminated and replaced by a slightly larger unit, the *arrondissement* or *poste administratif*.[28]

These changes are justified by the rulers as an attempt to decen-

---

[28] The present status of the *canton* in Senegal and the Ivory Coast is not very clear.

tralize administration and to bring it into closer contact with the administered at their own request. There is little doubt, indeed, that the inhabitants of many localities have welcomed the promotion of their *subdivision* into a *cercle,* or of their *canton* into a *poste administratif,* for example, because this normally means that important services such as post offices, agricultural extension, and even schools will be more substantial and within easier physical reach. At the same time, however, there is little doubt that this downward penetration represents a substantial increase in the center's potential for control over the localities. Whether this potential can be realized or not remains to be seen, since the personnel available to man these posts is usually inexperienced and very scarce; at any rate it does constitute an important way of objectifying the new political order, of giving substance to the concept of a modern state.

It is in the very nature of such a system of administration to have an important political component: in France, for example, the prefect during the nineteenth century was a man carefully selected for his loyalty to the central authority; only recently has there grown a corps of professional administrators to fill these posts.[29] In Africa, whether the individual appointed governor of a region (or regional commissioner, or prefect of a department) is formally a "party" or "government" man, his administrative skill is obviously less important than his political loyalty to the President (even when his formal chief happens to be the Minister of the Interior). This is confirmed by the usual absence of a distinct party official at that level and by the fact that there is always much movement and purging among such officials whenever a crisis occurs. Below, the dual system prevails: there are usually both administrators and party secretaries. In spite of their efforts to maintain this duality, however, most states have encountered serious difficulties because the population tends to view authority as diffuse rather than specific and hence to express loyalty to one or the other of these two officials, who themselves often compete for precedence. In order to eliminate actual and potential conflicts, the central authorities have often attempted to integrate the officials while preserving the distinction between them: thus in the Ivory Coast, Mali, and Guinea, the administrator was made an *ex officio* member of the appropriate *bureau politique* and in an emergency has even been called upon to act as interim secretary-general of the party branch. In Guinea,

---

[29]See Brian Chapman, *Introduction to French Local Government* (London: George Allen and Unwin, 1953), *passim.*

this has been reciprocated by appointing the secretary-general assistant to the administrator.

The Ivory Coast created and elected *conseils généraux* at the departmental level in 1959 and later advisory councils in each *sous-préfecture,* but these organs do not appear to be operational. Such regional councils did function in Guinea, but their tiny budgets suggest that they were quite unimportant. Mali originally intended to follow suit but abandoned the idea of formally elected regional councils and has instituted instead at each level the local equivalent of the national cadre conference, which includes party and government officials as well as popular representatives such as women, youth leaders, and "notabilities," i.e., individuals of high traditional status.

Except in a few areas such as the Fulani regions of Mali or Guinea, the Agni country in the Ivory Coast, or the Mossi region of Upper Volta, where they practiced a kind of indirect rule, the French paid relatively little attention to traditional norms in choosing *chefs de canton* and these chiefs were usually unpopular. As we saw earlier, national movements often arose specifically in opposition to their power and battled against competing parties for which these same chiefs provided the organizational basis. It is not surprising, therefore, to find that the dominant parties in each country were intent upon neutralizing the *chefs de canton* as early as possible. President Senghor long ago incorporated many of them into his political machine. In the Ivory Coast a genuine political purge began among them in 1952 and by 1959 most of them were pro-PDCI. Although in the latter year many party leaders would have liked to eliminate them from the administration altogether, the President judged that this was politically unnecessary and decided to avoid a frontal assault. Usually no successors are appointed when they die or retire, so that the system will phase itself out gradually. But the Ivoiriens sympathized with the decision made by Guinea in 1958 and by Mali the following year to eliminate them altogether, because in those two countries the *chefs de canton* continued to be anti-RDA and constituted a major obstacle to the achievement of the one-party state. In all four countries, however, certain chiefs who were sufficiently astute to have made their peace with the dominant party early in the game and who also have the required level of education (a very rare occurrence in French Africa!) have been appointed to minor administrative posts, in particular at the level of the *arrondissement.*

On the whole the village chiefs have retained their office, whether qua chiefs, as in the Ivory Coast, or as appointed presidents of elected village councils, as in many parts of Mali and Guinea. Unfortunately, little research has yet been done at this microcosmic level and it is impossible to generalize about politics in the village. In Mali, it seems that the village *administrative* committee is usually composed of traditional elders, while the village *party* committee is often controlled by the youth or by immigrants; some officials privately suggest that this constitutes a lively "two-party system." In Guinea, the village administrative committees which had been elected in 1958 were abolished in 1962 and their powers were given to the village party committee. What did this mean? In the light of Sékou Touré's comment quoted earlier for Conakry, possibly it means that there was so much overlap between the two that the differentiation had become meaningless.

Ghanaian political administration at the regional level (which replaced the older provinces) has been since 1957 in the hands of commissioners who are "party" men appointed by the President; they are seconded by a regional secretary, however, who is the senior civil servant in the area. In Ghana, much as in French-speaking Africa, the number of districts has been approximately doubled, and the regional arrangements are replicated at this lower level. The elected regional assemblies provided by the 1957 constitution at the request of the opposition were reduced to an advisory role in the course of the first major struggle between government and opposition after independence, and eventually abolished altogether; but on the other hand, district councils were created everywhere in 1962. Below them are village and town committees with members nominated by the district commissioners in consultation with CPP officials and chiefs.

That the chiefs participate in the governmental process may be surprising in the light of the widely publicized notion that the central government has waged a struggle against them since independence, but it becomes understandable if close attention is paid to what has really happened. Although the opposition had demanded a national second chamber for chiefs, this was not provided for in the 1957 constitution; instead, however, each region was provided with a House of Chiefs. Unlike the regional assemblies, they have continued to operate, albeit in an advisory role only. Attacks on chiefs since 1958 have been directed less against traditional authorities as such than against particular chiefs in particular regions where it was evident that the institution fostered opposition, as was the case in many parts of Ashanti, in Akim Abuakwa in the South, and eventually in some Ga areas around Accra.

In Ghana, as in the Ivory Coast, the central authorities have attempted to neutralize and co-opt chiefs. Thus, the Asantehene (paramount chief of Ashanti) has been treated with great deference ever since he came over to the government side; after a head-on clash with the CPP in 1958, the paramount chief of Akim Abuakwa backed President Nkrumah against his own kinsman, J. B. Danquah, in the 1960 Presidential elections; following another conflict in 1961, however, the Akim Abuakwa council was abolished. Beyond this, the government has undermined the economic position of chiefs, which had often been a steppingstone for political action, by taking control of the revenue from "stool lands."

Because Ghanaian chiefs are on the whole more educated and have had greater experience of administration than their French African counterparts, it has been easier for the government to incorporate them into the secular administration, where they now occupy a place similar to that of chiefs in French-speaking Africa *before* independence. How important chiefs remain in Ghana, however, can be seen from the 1958 decision that henceforth chiefs would rank below MP's and judges in the formal order of state precedence: although their status was reduced, it remains officially much higher than would be conceivable in any French-speaking African country.

It is perhaps in the towns that the direction of post-independence changes in government has been most visible. Guinea eliminated its recently created *communes* in 1959 and incorporated them into the administrative districts that surround them, allowing them to retain elected councils, but with government officials instead of elected mayors as chief municipal executives, thus returning to the pre-reform colonial system. The government of the Ivory Coast did not hesitate to suspend the mayor and to disband the municipal council of its third largest city in 1960 and to replace them with an appointed commission. The President himself was mayor of Abidjan for a long time; when he withdrew, he was succeeded by a safe political lieutenant. Municipal self-government was much more strongly anchored in the life of Senegal, where several *communes* have a history going back to the French Revolution. But precisely because of this they have retained their political autonomy and have long resisted the hegemony of President Senghor's party; the opposition was still able to make a very strong showing in two populous wards of the capital in 1961 and to foment trouble there in 1963. Hence, the Senegalese have begun to follow suit: several municipal councils were dissolved in 1963 and

Dakar was reorganized to strengthen control by the central government; there were no longer any opposition candidates in the municipal elections of 1964; and further reforms in the same direction were expected in 1965.

Because municipalities have sometimes acted as opposition strongholds in Ghana as well, the central government there has also repeatedly suspended the municipal councils of Kumasi and Accra. That this was necessary even after they had become thoroughly CPP-controlled provides, incidentally, a further revelation of the looseness of party discipline and loyalty. Accra was eventually enlarged to include its surrounding territory and a high-ranking official was appointed by the President as its administrator.

In most of these cases the growth of central control over cities, and in particular over the capital, is apparently motivated by fear of opposition. This can be easily understood in the light of the political history of Western Europe or even of the United States, where it took nearly two centuries to extend the concept of "grass-roots democracy" to include self-government in the capital because of the ancient fear of popular pressures on the central government this might entail. It is evident, however, that the tendency to reduce urban self-government is not motivated solely by these fears, but that it is due also to a serious concern with corruption. There have been recent attempts in Ghana to professionalize local government employees and to create an inspectorate over local government directly responsible to the President. Announcing this and other measures, the Minister of Local Government recently enjoined the district commissioners and the members of local councils to stop viewing councils as private money-making concerns and warned them to stop pocketing special levies they had been collecting for worthless and bogus contracts. Corruption and inefficiency are less tolerable in a new country where resources are very scarce than in one where they are so abundant that corruption and waste at the local level can be tolerated as the price of maintaining "grass-roots democracy."

THE CIVIL SERVICE

It is evident by now that whatever importance is attached to the party in West Africa, governmental bureaucracies continue to be a major instrument of rule. The challenge which all regimes have faced in this sphere are very serious, not only because of the absolute shortage of qualified personnel—a question which will not be discussed here —but especially because of problems of political loyalty and effectiveness which stem from the norms that prevail among the personnel available to man the bureaucracy now and in the future.

These problems have been referred to in connection with other items and now need be only briefly summarized. In French-speaking Africa, government employees had provided cadre for the dominant movement as well as for its opponents: it appears on the whole that those who worked in very close contact with French political administrators tended to be most vulnerable to colonial pressures and were usually found in the ranks of the *partis de l'administration* along with the *chefs de canton;* on the other hand, low-level clerks were particularly prone to be active among the more radical labor unions which in the mid-1950's began to oppose the moderate policies of the nationalist leadership. In Ghana the Africans in the civil service, because they were better trained and had achieved higher positions, were also likely to have internalized British norms and hence to deplore the replacement of British administrators by African politicians.

Thus, at the time of independence, there prevailed in many countries a generalized suspicion between politicians and civil servants. President Nkrumah's pronouncement on this matter was characteristic of the thinking of many other rulers:

> Civil servants, particularly those in the higher grades, should maintain a political neutrality and give completely loyal service to the duly constituted Government, regardless of its political complexion .... It is our intention to tighten up the regulations and to wipe out the disloyal elements in the civil service, even if by so doing we suffer some temporary dislocation of the service. ... For disloyal civil servants are not better than saboteurs.[30]

In the same speech, he also deplored slovenly attitudes toward work, echoing French-speaking African complaints about the widespread absence of *conscience professionelle* among government employees, and generalized concern everywhere with inefficiency and corruption. It is not, of course, that politicians are more efficient and less corrupt than administrators, but rather that the outlook of the politicians changed in this respect as well as in others when they

---

[30] Kwame Nkrumah, *I Speak of Freedom: A Statement of African Ideology* (New York: Praeger, 1961), p. 173.

assumed executive responsibilities. Furthermore, it is also possible that self-selection into one or the other group had occurred: those educated Africans who had become nationalist politicians may have been on the whole more innovative, while those who chose to continue their career primarily as employees of the colonial government were more routine-oriented and hence fit the politicians' stereotype of the conservative-minded bureaucrat.[31]

It is again to the party that the rulers have turned to carry out the task of instilling into government employees as well as the population at large an ethic of honesty, hard work, and achievement. This has led to an effort to incorporate civil servants into the party, or at least to provide in their midst party cells which will help replace "selfish individualism" by "patriotic socialism." How difficult that is to accomplish can be seen from the complaint voiced by a Malien official that such party cells spent so many office-hours trying to persuade employees to come to work on time that the bureaucratic output of many offices had been drastically reduced! Furthermore, the results of these efforts are doubtful because they are being made while many governments are distributing negative rewards to their employees, i.e., cuts in privileges inherited from the colonial period, such as paid vacations abroad, and sometimes even salary cuts to help alleviate the immense burdens on the budget. The struggle against corruption is also very frustrating since the punishment meted out tends to deprive the government of the service of individuals who, however corrupt, nevertheless performed *some* work and sometimes cannot be replaced with equally qualified men.

In many West African states, bureaucrats have become scapegoats for the failure of various programs because the only alternative explanations would be that the programs had been poorly conceived by the rulers themselves or that no program could possibly succeed. This feeling sometimes merges into a more generalized anti-intellectualism which also affects attitudes toward the civil servants of the future who are now students. It is this sense of frustration, perhaps more than any specific ideological conflict, which underlies President Nkrumah's attacks on the University of Ghana, as when he warned in 1959 that

---

[31]This hypothesis, completely untested so far, is inspired by the parallel differentiation among the military stressed by Morris Janowitz in *The Military in the Political Development of New Nations* (Chicago: University of Chicago Press, 1964), pp. 44–49, in which he distinguishes between "prescribed" or "routine" as against "adaptive" careers.

it must "cease being an alien institution" and that "no resort to a cry of academic freedom (for academic freedom does not mean academic irresponsibility) is going to restrain us from seeing that our University is a healthy, Ghanaian University, devoted to Ghanaian interests."[32] Criticism of the wearing of imperialist academic gowns by students and of their unsocialistic ivory-towerish orientation often appeared in the party press in later years. The climax came with the symbolic invasion of the campus by CPP activists in 1964 and the deportation of six expatriate faculty members.

These attacks on the more educated men in the country, which are common also in French-speaking Africa, are evocative of an aspect of popular politics encountered in many other polities: faced with the great unknown, politicians are frustrated because they believe that somehow intellectuals possess a secret knowledge which could help unlock mysteries, but which they refuse to share. Lest the Ghanaian situation in particular be misunderstood, it must be noted that the University of Ghana is entirely government-supported, much like an American state university, and that in addition the students who attend it are fully supported by the government for the entire course of their studies. The analogy of the American state university may perhaps be extended to the conflict itself, which is remindful—*mutatis mutandis*—of the tense relationship which often prevails between relatively conservative state legislatures and state-supported institutions which they consider to be hotbeds of liberalism. Within this context, the recent decision of the Ghana government to review scholarship awards annually on the basis of good conduct and satisfactory performance has a familiar ring. But we are immediately reminded that this is West Africa by the concurrent announcement that all entering students as well as those going to study abroad, must first spend two weeks of indoctrination at the CPP Ideological Institute at Winneba!

THE MERGER OF PARTY AND GOVERNMENT

Do the institutional transformations visible toward the end of the first decade indicate a major common trend among the one-party states of West Africa studied here, or do there appear to be significant variations? In particular, is it useful to distinguish between a "pragmatic-

---

[32]*Tenth Anniversary Speech of 1959*, p. 31.

pluralistic" (or "reconciliation") trend and a "revolutionary-centralizing" (or "mobilization") tendency?[33] Since these tendencies refer to both ideological and organizational aspects, the attempt to answer the question provides an opportunity to draw together the observations made in the last three chapters.

As they engaged in the pursuit of their goals—the realization of unity, the affirmation of a political identity, the creation of a rational order, and generally speaking the modernization of the entire society—the rulers of the new West African states had at their disposal two major instruments. With some variation from country to country, the party was initially a loose movement which naturally incorporated the characteristics of the society in which it grew; it was eventually transformed into a political machine but continued to reflect the state of incomplete integration of the territorial society. Yet it was the most concrete expression of the nation, it was a self-made indigenous institution, and it was an instrument with which the new rulers were familiar. The government, in contrast, was an alien institution, manned until recently exclusively by Europeans and run according to strange bureaucratic norms. It was designed to be operated economically with a minimal staff of experts at the top and was geared to perform relatively limited services rather than to transform society. Yet it was the most concrete expression of central authority available, and it was an instrument which was known to be reliable.

While adapting these instruments to new needs, the new rulers were faced with the task of defining and implementing a relationship between them. The solution in each case can be viewed as the result of an interaction between the ideological preferences discussed in Chapter II and the constraints stemming from the structural characteristics of party and governmental apparatuses as well as from certain aspects of the social environment within which political processes occurred.

Initially there appeared to be a significant contrast between two types of solutions. Thus, while Guinea and Mali successively attempted

---

[33]The "pragmatic-pluralistic" and "revolutionary-centralizing" distinction is discussed by Coleman and Rosberg, pp. 4–6, and 671ff. The "mobilization" and "reconciliation" distinction appeared in a slightly different form in David Apter and Carl Rosberg, Jr., "Nationalism and Models of Political Change in Africa," *The Political Economy of Contemporary Africa* ("Symposia Studies Series 1," National Institute of Social and Behavioral Science, George Washington University, 1959), and in David Apter, *The Politics of Modernization* (Chicago: University of Chicago Press, 1965), pp. 357–421.

to survive with almost no qualified personnel to man the higher ranks of their civil service, the party became by default the most effective multifunctional political institution available. Its prominence was further enhanced when, in the course of legitimizing the decisions that had led to the current predicament, the leaders of these states stressed the break with the recent past and the country's rebirth through the mediation of the party. The leaders' stated intentions and their own account of what was happening in the political and the economic sphere, expressed in a rhetoric replete with the imagery of mobilization and struggle, which owed much to the Soviet model, were the main sources of information available to observers. These statements indeed constituted the most salient aspect of the entire political process, from which students of African politics inferred enduring characteristics of the regime.

The image of Senegal, and especially of the Ivory Coast, was very different. These two countries became independent with the consent of France; expatriate civil servants continued to man the governmental bureaucracy while Africans were being trained to replace them; there were few changes of direction in the economic sphere; the party tended to retain the machine style developed earlier. Perhaps in order to reassure potential private investors and other sources of aid, the extension of control by the central authorities over various aspects of social and political life tended to be justified as *ad hoc* measures for the maintenance of law and order rather than as the result of ideological imperatives in the name of the party. Here again, the self-image created by the country tended to be accepted by observers. The case of Ghana, as usual, was more ambiguous. Because its political process was more closely scrutinized by students of African politics than that of the other countries under discussion, the difficulties of fitting Ghana into one or the other of these nascent categories were evident. It shared the rhetoric of Guinea and Mali, but also many features of Senegal and of the Ivory Coast, and was characterized by swings from one political mood to another.

With the benefit of a few additional years of experience, however, we can begin to correct these images. These years are important because they constitute a period during which the constraints under which the rulers of these states operate have become much more visible to them and to us. We know now that beyond specific preferences for a party-dominant as against a government-dominant system, or for one approach to economic development over another, there lies a common political ideology which stresses effectiveness and order above all, and that order itself is defined as self-maintenance of the incumbents. Faced with this persistent problem and the recurrent challenges to their authority, the rulers tend to use the most convenient and reliable means available. Although in Guinea and Mali they initially stressed the party, only some of the individuals to whom high governmental posts were assigned on the basis of political loyalty have remained loyal and have become effective administrators. These survive and are being professionalized; as the bureaucracy expands, key positions are being filled by a growing number of qualified administrators.[34] In Ghana and in the Ivory Coast, where the crisis of the party has been most severe and many party men have been eliminated, the central authorities have most clearly come to rely on a small group of men who are not organizationally associated with the party but who are loyal. In the Ivory Coast it is even possible for technocrats to be given high party responsibilities as well. There is thus a common tendency toward the emergence of regimes in which governmental and administrative structures are at least as salient as parties. This trend will probably be accentuated because the leadership ranks of all the dominant parties consist of a relatively homogeneous political generation (regardless of biological age) which is quite fearful of invasion by younger, more educated men. For the latter, the only alternative path to prestige and power (other than all-out opposition) is the administration. Within a short time, therefore, it is likely that these regimes will be composed of a senescent party and of a young, vigorous governmental bureaucracy which will not hesitate to assert its place in the sun.

At the same time, the distinction between party and government has become blurred at the highest and at the lowest levels, but for different reasons. At the top, the tendency toward executive centralization and monocephalism has resulted in a concentration of authority in the hands of a single man operating through lieutenants, some of whom can be labeled "party" and others "government," but who usually owe whatever authority they have to their chief. At the bottom, in spite of efforts to maintain separate lines of communication and distinct

---

[34]Ghana announced in 1962 that the district commissioners (political appointees) would be given intensive training in local council administration to help them to supervise and direct the councils. (*West Africa*, November 24, 1962.) There are institutes of public administration in Mali and Guinea which turn out career men or retrain party officials who were rapidly promoted but lack adequate formal education to function effectively.

structures of authority, all these lines are confused because in the eyes of the population it is impossible to be loyal to two "modern chiefs." Whether in any given case the government or the party official is more authoritative seems to be less determined by ideological directives or by their respective institutional affiliation than by their relative ability to carry out their assigned tasks and to construct a local coalition to obtain support.

Even where the domain of party activity continues to include most aspects of political, social, and economic life, the party is used much less as a parallel structure of ideological control over administrative institutions than as an auxiliary task force to make up for their inadequacies. Party militants who help collect taxes, carry out censuses, announce governmental directives, and perform police work in Mali are much more reminiscent of all-purpose sheriff's deputies than of Soviet guardians. In reverse, where parties appear to fail in their performance of important control tasks, it is not unusual to find administrators stepping in. In the Ivory Coast policemen may be deployed to check on whether individuals have paid their party dues and government officials play an important role in the management of elections. Everywhere a large proportion of the cost of party activities is borne directly or indirectly by the public budget.

In all five countries, the party-government complex has been extended in such a way as to assert more firmly than ever before the existence of a state which claims authority over the territory. On the whole the government continues to function much as it had done during the colonial period, as a centralized and hierarchical system of administration. The party remains the more popular institution. Nowhere has it been successfully transformed into an effective instrument of mobilization. Often to the dismay of the central authorities, it continues to reflect the society in which it has grown and to act as a major mechanism for the expression of demands. Nevertheless, it is also serviceable as a sort of public relations agency for the central authorities, explaining in popular language why what the rulers and their technical advisers, Africans or Europeans, Frenchmen or Russians, have decided to do must be done. The party can tell the public much better than the government itself that the state is no longer an alien presence, but that it represents a new indigenous political order; that they must therefore obey its directives and work hard. Usually the party does this in the manner of a teacher in an old-fashioned classroom: it enunciates truths before the class, saying "Repeat after me," using gold stars for rewards and dealing blows as punishment.

It is therefore more useful to view "mobilization" and "reconciliation" as concepts which refer to aspects of the political process in each of these countries rather than as mutually exclusive tendencies. What appeared to be sharp contrasts between the "pragmatic-pluralistic pattern" and the "revolutionary-centralizing trend" a few years ago have been considerably blunted, as even the originators of the conceptual distinction suggest.[35] Although a new term, "no-party state," is beginning to gain some currency, this reflects primarily the disappointed hopes of those who expected parties to successfully transform African societies within a short time. It exaggerates the nadir much as the earlier concepts exaggerated the zenith. It is not African parties that have changed so much, but rather our appreciation of the difficulties of political modernization. For the time being, given the partnership between party and government that is visible everywhere, to suggest that the common features of these countries are very significant, and to remind us that the characteristics of these regimes stem from shared environments and circumstances, it is useful to speak simply of "the West African party-state."

[35] Coleman and Rosberg, p. 671.

CHAPTER V

THE PARTY-STATE IN PERSPECTIVE

ALTHOUGH IN THE PRECEDING CHAPTERS THE EMPHASIS HAS BEEN ON THE common characteristics of the regimes of the five countries studied, we have remained very close to empirical reality and operated at a relatively low level of generalization in order to sketch a somewhat detailed and fairly realistic composite portrait of the West African party-state. Given the misconceptions that prevail in much of the literature on this subject, our main purpose has been frankly revisionist. Nevertheless, in order to round out the analysis and suggest the beginnings of an alternative approach to the study of African politics, we shall now attempt to view the West African party-state at a somewhat higher level of generalization. This chapter will therefore adopt the vantage point of the society in which the party-state operates, raise some questions concerning the relationship of the party-state to the political system of that society, and conclude by introducing the perspective of time.

THE PERSPECTIVE OF THE POLITICAL SYSTEM

The level of generalization at which we now attempt to view the politics of the five West African countries under scrutiny approximates that of the political system as conceptualized by David Easton, which is "the most inclusive system of behavior in a society for the authoritative allocation of values."[1] Therefore, instead of merely analyzing the structure of the party-state, as we have done so far, we shall attempt to provide at least a sketchy answer to the following questions about

---

[1] David Easton, *A Framework for Political Analysis* (Englewood Cliffs, N.J.: Prentice-Hall, 1965), p. 56.

West African countries: "How are values authoritatively allocated for the society?" and "What role does the party-state play in this allocative activity?" The usefulness of the systemic perspective becomes clear because of immediate difficulties we encounter in answering. Usually, political scientists who speak of political systems have in mind at least implicitly the context of an identifiable concrete society, be it contemporary Great Britain or a small tribe of highland Burma or northern Togo. It is more difficult, however, after a moment of reflection, to take as a given the existence of a "society" which encompasses all the individuals living within the territorial confines of any of the five countries under consideration here.

A century ago or less, there existed on the African continent, within the area encompassed today by any of the five countries (or by all of them and their neighbors as a group), a large number of societies varying in size, in social structure, and in culture, each with a corresponding political system. They also varied from relatively undifferentiated ones in which political and kinship structures were almost indistinguishable to highly differentiated ones usually referred to as "states." They did not exist in isolation but constantly interacted so as to warrant the designation of the area as an international political system, or, if we wish to relate the area to the world at large, as a regional subsystem of the international system.[2] The relationships between the individual political actors within the subsystem and those between the subsystem as a whole, or some of its parts, and the international system, varied greatly over time. About a century ago, however, certain international actors (principally France and Great Britain) extended the boundaries of their own political community to include some of the societies of the African continent.

The definition of new political units such as "Senegal," "French West Africa," or "Gold Coast," did not, of course, result automatically in the creation of a new society within these legally defined territorial boundaries. There is no doubt that initially at least the various societies caught within the net cast over a particular geographical area retained their identity. The changes that occurred, however, particularly affected their individual political systems, as well as the interactions between them that constituted the regional international subsystem. What form these changes took constitutes the major theme in the political history of the colonial period. It ranged from the limiting case of almost com-

---

[2] For a conceptualization of the international system, see Morton A. Kaplan, *System and Process in International Politics* (New York: John Wiley & Sons, 1957).

plete preservation of an African political system and the establishment of a federal type of relationship between it and the European system (as in a pure type of indirect rule), to the complete destruction of the African political system and an extension of the European political system over the corresponding society (as in a pure type of direct rule). In practice, however, neither of these limiting cases was ever met.

During the past three or four decades, the impact of cultural, social, economic, and political change has been heightened. A growing number of Africans who were members of particular societies began to interact across the boundaries of these societies. At the same time the colonial power developed its central bureaucracy, territorial political organizations began to appear. Thus it could be said that a new territorial society was in the making and that corresponding to this incipient society there arose an incipient political system. Nevertheless, although Africans have taken control of the central bureaucracy, it is reasonable to assume that the pre-existing African societies and their corresponding political system have not totally disappeared. Hence, any consideration of the authoritative allocation of values in countries such as these must come to grips with the persisting duality of political processes.

This duality of societies and of political systems coexisting within the territorial boundaries of new states can be grasped intuitively, but it is difficult to express it with conceptual precision. Although it may be useful for some purposes to adopt a conceptual approach which views each country as being composed of numerous interacting societies, and hence to consider the territorial political process as merely the sum of the interactions within and between the political systems it contains, this approach takes us very far afield and necessitates the abandonment of most of the available conceptual apparatus of comparative politics. Before adopting it, other alternatives should be considered. It is also possible to assume that to each new country there corresponds a single, albeit imperfectly integrated, society, and also, by definition, a single political system dealing with the authoritative allocation of values for that society. Unless this is qualified, however, it leads to a loss of the intuitive grasp we have acquired of the duality of the political process.

While adopting this approach, the duality could be retained and even made operational by classifying individuals living in these countries into two or more appropriate political categories. Karl Deutsch, for example, has distinguished, on the basis of degree of political participation and exposure to political communications, two sets in any population, the "mobilized" and the "non-mobilized"³ Following a similar procedure, Daniel Lerner has distinguished between "moderns," "transitionals," and "traditionals."⁴ But this sort of approach raises a serious conceptual difficulty, in addition to the practical problems stemming from the difficulty of distinguishing between participants and non-participants in countries where the government is intent on demonstrating unanimity. Although it is a heuristic device to help us understand the process of national political integration, it can tell us mostly whether or not and at what rate this process is occurring. It tells us very little about the vital problem before us, namely, *what the political system of an unintegrated country is like,* and tends to gloss over the fact that even the individuals who are not "mobilized" participate in politics *of some sort.*

We can avoid the problem of struggling with the notion of multisocietal states and still retain the sense of political duality by stressing the "allocation of values" aspect of Easton's definition of the political system. It is possible to suggest that the *values* that are authoritatively allocated in West African countries can be classified into two categories, one set to be called "modern" and the other—avoiding the word "traditional," which will be reserved for another purpose—to be called simply "residual." Furthermore, it is also possible to distinguish analytically between political structures that deal with authoritative allocation of the first set and others that deal with the second. We can then speak of a political system with two sectors, the one modern, the other residual. Since this an analytical distinction, it can be stated also that any member of the political system occupies more or less important roles in *both* sectors. Although some individuals are more active in the one than in the other, these roles are not mutually exclusive. It is not only analytically possible, but empirically probable that we shall find individuals who occupy important roles in both sectors at the same time, while it is not possible to speak of someone who is *both* politically mobilized and non-mobilized without substantially modifying Deutsch's approach.⁵

The applicability of the distinction of two political sectors to the

---
³Karl A. Deutsch, "Social Mobilization and Political Development," *American Political Science Review,* LV, No. 3 (September, 1961), 492–514.
⁴Daniel Lerner, *The Passing of Traditional Society* (Glencoe, Ill.: The Free Press, 1958), *passim.*
⁵Deutsch, does, of course, distinguish between mobilization in various sectors (political, economic, etc.), but within a given sector, an individual can only be inside or outside the set.

West African countries with which we are concerned and the consequences for the understanding of their politics can be illustrated as follows. If we wish to examine, for example, the activities of the party-state in the economic sphere, with which it is greatly concerned and where it is well known that it desires to play a determining role in value-allocation (through state entrepreneurship, regulation of economic activity, taxation, redistribution of income, etc.), we can take as one rough index the proportion that the total annual budget represents of the estimated GNP. The figure we obtain is in the range of 15 to 25 per cent, with the Ivory Coast and Ghana in the lower range and the remaining countries in the upper.[6] The significance of these figures is highlighted by Deutsch's finding that the budget of richer, non-Communist countries in the mid-1950's averaged about 30 per cent of the GNP. This somewhat surprising result can be understood once we take into account the fact that although the party-state plays an important role in the relatively modern economic sector (monetary transactions, import-export, industry), this sector itself is only a part of the total economic system. Much of what goes into the computation of GNP is in a residual sector, including subsistence agriculture and husbandry, locally marketed products, and even traditional imports and exports such as cattle, fish, kola nuts, and salt, which follow century-old trade routes. Most of the economic activity in this sector, which varies in importance from country to country, is, practically speaking, outside the domain of the party-state's allocative authority, even when it claims the legal right to make decisions that affect it.[7] Yet there can be no doubt that in this residual sector rules and regulations exist, together with authoritative agencies to settle disputes, change rules, enforce obligations, etc.[8]

The distinction applies even more strikingly, albeit in a less tangible manner, to the entire sphere of norms and regulations relating to

---

[6]The economic indicators used in this entire chapter are very sketchy, and they are used for illustrative purposes only; GNP and per capita income are from AID, as reprinted in *Africa Report*, VIII, No. 3 (August, 1963); budgets for French-speaking countries are taken from figures published in *Europe-France-Outremer*, No. 397 (May, 1963).

[7]Malien officials, for example, estimated that the country's traditional exports were much greater than its "modern" exports and produced a net surplus in trade, but the government cannot "reach" this income in any way.

[8]For traditional economic activity, see, for example, Paul Bohannan and George Dalton (eds.), *Markets in Africa* (Garden City, N.Y.: Doubleday and Co., 1965).

personal status. The inclusion of this apparently private sphere in the political system is so well established in modern societies that it is thought of as non-political. But such activities as the registration of births and deaths, the enforcement of rules concerning marriage and divorce, the definition of personal rights, the inheritance of property, the regulation of work, are clearly important areas of policy-making, as the consideration of the political history of any of these items or the recurrent debate over some of them (segregation, birth control) quickly reminds us. It is therefore highly significant to note that the activities of the West African party-state in this entire sphere are extremely limited. The regime is concerned with extending its authority in this direction by making laws that will affect these activities, but of course, there is a vast difference between the staking of a claim to do so and the genuine operation of allocative authority. Yet, perhaps even more than in the sphere of residual economic activity, we know that rules exist, that they are enforced, that they undergo change, that conflicts occur, and that they are settled, hence that the political system allocates values authoritatively in this sphere.

The party-state thus deals primarily with the authoritative allocation of one set of values; in a sense, its activities do not fill the entire political system of the society in which it operates. We can adopt as a working hypothesis that there is a residual political space which is filled by other structures. The fact that political activity in this sector is not immediately visible to us does not mean that it is unimportant or irrelevant, but rather, as we have indicated earlier, that the conceptual apparatus of political scientists and other observers leads them to gather information of a certain type only. What we do not see, however, is at least as important for our understanding as what we do see. How then are these residual values allocated? In countries where traditional political structures have been assigned a legitimate role—such as in Nigeria or in Uganda, for example—the answer is relatively obvious. Although it is more difficult to imagine what occurs in countries such as Mali or Guinea, where traditional rulers have been deprived of all legal authority, we know that only a limited amount of allocative activity is carried out by the party-state. The most likely answer is therefore that traditional structures still perform extremely important political functions. It is noteworthy in this respect that a similar hypothesis was advanced nearly forty years ago by Raymond Buell, who remarked, when discussing the role of chiefs in French Africa, that although these chiefs had a lesser official role in the judiciary than they were given in British Africa, their actual authority may have been greater because it was unchecked by the colonial authorities.[9]

The verification of the working hypothesis proposed here requires research that has not yet been carried out. Meanwhile, however, the view of the political system it suggests reveals the paradox of the party-state. An examination of West African politics which is concerned only with the modern sector easily leads to a characterization of the political process as one in which a single political organization has achieved a monopoly of authority. The alternative approach recognizes the importance of this feature but stresses that it is an incomplete characterization since much of the political activity that is carried on in the society remains outside the modern sector. It enables us to understand how it is possible to suggest that the party-state is authoritarian within its domain, but that at the same time this domain is very limited, and that on the whole the regime has little authority. Thus, while it is perhaps appropriate to speak of the "one-party state," at the level of the political system there are other authorities than the rulers of the party-state, and hence it is misleading to speak of a "one-party system."

THE NATURE OF AUTHORITY IN THE PARTY-STATE

If we now re-examine the political patterns discussed in previous chapters the general trends appear to be as follows. First, the party-state is attempting to expand the domain of its authority to encompass a broader sector of the political system. It is doing so by extending its party and governmental apparatus to reach farther down into the society and farther out to distant regions, or as they put it in Mali, by weaving a dense spider's web. It is also extending its domain by making rules in spheres of human activity hitherto outside the sphere of modern politics. How successful the party-state has been in achieving these goals is difficult to estimate. We know, however, that realities seldom correspond to the intent of the rulers. The announcement by an African government that an institution such as chieftaincy has been abolished, that a new one such as a network of village party committees has been established, that older norms have given way to new ones, must not be taken as an indication that the old no longer exists

---

[9]Raymond Buell, *The Native Problem in Africa* (New York: Macmillan, 1927), I, 1000.

or that the new is operational above a minimal level. On the whole, such announcements are indicative of a change of norms at one level of the political system, but not necessarily in the norms and structures that prevail throughout much as even in a very modern polity such as the United States, Supreme Court decisions declaring segregated schools unconstitutional, however significant, cannot be used as evidence even ten years later that segregated schools are no longer a characteristic feature of the American society. In Africa, much more than in the United States, such announcements can seldom be adequately checked against realities and must therefore be evaluated on the basis of experiential rules of thumb founded on tough-minded skepticism. Nevertheless, it is true that the efforts of the party-state in this direction have borne some fruit.

The second major trend suggests a steady drive to achieve greater centralization of authority in the hands of a very small number of men who occupy top offices in the party and the government, and even more in the hands of a single man at the apex of both institutions. Since the opposition was eliminated, the major source of political tension has stemmed from the contest between the paramount leader and important lieutenants, as well as between the center and regional officials in the apparatus. How successful the top leadership has been in this respect is also difficult to evaluate. Whether he acts primarily through the party or through the government, the top leader has been able on the whole to consolidate his position by making sure that subordinate leaders who have a power base in specific regions are effectively restricted to these regions, while his own personal authority is beginning to rest on a territorial base; he has also acquired a great deal of leverage by creating multiple chains of command which coexist in a state of tension. Nevertheless, negative evidence such as the top leaders' recurrent admonitions concerning lack of discipline, the persistence of regionalism, and the pursuit of selfish interests, suggests that in spite of all efforts, the party-state retains a great measure of decentralization, with relatively autonomous subordinate authorities.

At the present level of generalization, the spectacle of the expansion of the domain of the state's authority into new fields, of the struggle between the center and the regions, and of the tension between a supreme leader and his lieutenants, is by no means visible only in the West African party-state, or in the strikingly similar case of Tanzania. A very similar drama is taking place in African countries where federal arrangements and numerous parties prevail, as in Uganda or

Nigeria; in states dominated by a party which has never acquired a "mass" character, as in Niger; and even in spectacular fashion, with recurrent failures and continuing suspense, in the Congo. It is a continuation everywhere of the process which began with the establishment of a central administration by the European conquerors over newly defined political units during the colonial era. It also resembles the process which Lloyd Fallers believes led to the transformation of Buganda society into the Buganda kingdom in Uganda. Pointing out that African political systems were most commonly composed of segments and that the unilineal descent group was the basic building block of society, he states that "it provided a foundation for local corporateness and autonomy which stood in the way of greater centralization and royal despotism. Highly centralized states like Buganda could develop only by suppressing this autonomy . . . ."[10]

Fallers goes on to suggest that

> One is reminded . . . of Max Weber's discussion of feudalism and 'patrimonialism' in medieval European history—the struggle between the centralizing efforts of kings, expressed in their attempts to build up bodies of patrimonial retainers responsible to themselves alone and the decentralizing tendency of subordinate authorities to become locally rooted hereditary lords.[11]

A similar feeling of *déjà vu* is evoked when one contemplates the behavior of the top leaders in the West African party-states. In a revision of his book on Ghana, Apter characterizes Kwame Nkrumah in 1962–63 as a "Presidential monarch."[12] Nowhere, perhaps, is the historical parallel with Europe as striking as in Mali, where Modibo Keita has appointed a set of regional governors directly responsible to him in his capacity as President, and also a set of roving party commissioners directly responsible to him as Secretary-General of the *Union Soudanaise*. In addition, he spends about one-quarter of every year touring the regions with a suite consisting of party officials, elected representatives, and important bureaucrats. He holds court at daybreak in towns and villages, learning about local conditions, teach-

---

[10] Lloyd Fallers, *The King's Men* (London: Oxford University Press, 1964), p. 99. Reprinted by permission of the East African Institute of Social Research.

[11] *Ibid*. Professor Jan Vansina has suggested broadening this universe to include pre-European Morocco and Ethiopia during certain phases of its history.

[12] David Apter, *The Gold Coast in Transition* (Princeton: Princeton University Press, 1955), pp. 331, 337.

ing the population concepts of national citizenship, and making sure that the authority of his office is clearly understood to be tangible and paramount. He encourages the population to bring to his attention a variety of complaints, including grievances stemming from abuses committed by administrators or party officials, and settles village or town disputes that have been held in abeyance for years. In spite of the use of modern Marxist phraseology, the mood is akin to that of premodern Europe. But where does this analogy lead us? Is it merely an entertaining historical parallel, or does it contain a serious clue to the understanding of the West African party-state?

Beyond drawing attention to similarities in the behavior of rulers, the parallel suggests possible fundamental similarities in the very nature of the systems of authority which characterize these otherwise very different polities. It invites an inquiry into the legitimacy on which the authority of the rulers of the West African party-state rests.

In Weber's now classical formulation, no regime can rely on coercion alone: "In general, it should be kept clearly in mind that the basis of every system of authority, and correspondingly of every kind of willingness to obey, is a *belief,* a belief by virtue of which persons exercising authority are lent prestige."[13] It is the examination of the variety of such beliefs that led Weber to the construction of three major types of "imperative coordination" or of "domination," based upon three corresponding bases of legitimacy: the legal-rational, the charismatic, and the traditional.[14] Before attempting to consider the West African party-state in this light, however, we must remember Weber's own admonition that "The composition of this belief is seldom altogether simple."[15] Even legal authority—the system which prevails in the United States, for example—contains traditional elements (as with the Constitution and the Presidency, hallowed by time and tradition) but also a charismatic element "at least in the negative sense that persistent and striking lack of success may be sufficient to ruin any government, to undermine its prestige, and to prepare the way for charismatic revolution."[16]

---

[13] Max Weber, *The Theory of Social and Economic Organization* (New York: The Free Press, 1957), p. 382.

[14] For a general background to the problem under discussion, see *ibid.,* part III, "The Types of Authority and Imperative Coordination," especially pp. 324–86; also Reinhard Bendix, *Max Weber: An Intellectual Portrait* (London: Heinemann, 1960), pp. 289–368.

[15] Weber, *The Theory* . . . , p. 382.

[16] *Ibid.*

If these beliefs can co-exist, how can they form the basis for distinguishing between classes of polities? It might be useful to consider them as traits distributed according to varying patterns among the members of any political system, possibly even cumulatively, rather than as mutually exclusive sets in which the dominance of one type of belief necessarily implies the absence of others. Systems can then be characterized as clusterings of legitimacy variables and it would be possible to understand how the salience of these types of beliefs can vary over time within the same system, denoting important changes at the level of the regime.[17] With this in mind we can approach the question of the legitimacy of the "modern" set of authorities in the party-state.

Apter's fundamental insight concerning the charismatic nature of the authority of the leader of the nationalist movement in Ghana is useful as an initial proposition and can be extended to include leaders elsewhere. Some qualifications are needed, however. First the term "charismatic," which has rapidly entered into popular usage to refer to some general quality of flamboyance recognizable even by non-members of a particular system, has led to serious confusion exemplified by debates as to whether this or that African leader is "charismatic." It is obviously difficult for a American visitor meeting a man of small stature, wearing a conservatively cut Continental suit, drinking lemonade brought in by a frock-coated usher into his air-conditioned office, to feel mesmerized by President Houphouet-Boigny, but there is absolutely no doubt that this man is believed by many of his countrymen to be among the elect, specially designated to rule over them, and that it is on the basis of this belief that many of them have obeyed him for nearly twenty years. Thus, it is the relationship rather than objective qualities that counts. Second, "charisma" must be extended from a reference to a single leader's relationship with his followers to include the whole set of such relationships which provided the basis of legitimacy for the early nationalist movements. Typically, roles were not clearly defined, collegiality was important, gifts and hospitality were all-important forms of support, and at the height of the movement's activity many leaders had no other regular occupation, often because they had become ineligible for employment in schools or in the colonial bureaucracy because of their political activities. "CPP" and "RDA" became names to conjure with rather than mere party labels,

---

[17] I am particularly grateful to Professor David Easton for his suggestions concerning this section.

as illustrated by the fact that the success of the RDA in Mali was partly due, according to one qualified observer, to the favorable outcome of the arithmetic sum of the numerical values of the Arabic equivalents of the three letters which compose the party's initials.[18] The Mahdist tradition in Islam, as well as the messianic tradition in Christianity, contributed to the reinforcement of these beliefs. Third, however important this type of belief may have been, it coexisted from the very beginning with other types. For many individuals who had begun to internalize European norms, the legitimacy of these new men was based on democratic values. Furthermore, in most cases leaders and movements also stressed their relationship to pre-European states and movements and claimed to embody hallowed traditions.

During the period of militancy or "positive action," which occurred early in the Ivory Coast and Ghana, but much later in Guinea and Mali, the charismatic aspects of legitimacy were most salient because they were especially compatible with the future-oriented outlook of nationalist movements. Within a short time, however, these movements became ruling organizations concerned to a considerable extent with institution-building and self-maintenance. During this later period, the charismatic basis of legitimacy is no longer sufficient. In Weber's terminology, charismatic authority must be "routinized" if the system of domination is to last. For Weber, the major motive for routinization is

> naturally the striving for security. This means legitimization, on the one hand, of positions of authority and social prestige, on the other hand, of the economic advantages enjoyed by the followers and sympathizers of the leader. Another important motive, however, lies in the objective necessity of adaptation of the patterns of order and of the organization of the administrative staff to the normal, everyday needs and conditions of carrying on administration.[19]

Furthermore, "it is not possible for the costs of permanent, routine administration to be met by 'booty,' contributions, gifts and hospitality, as is typical of the pure type of military and prophetic charisma."[20] One is reminded here of the great stress placed by African leaders on the regular payment of party dues and appropriate taxes after self-

---

[18] Vincent Monteil, *L'Islam Noir* (Paris: Editions du Seuil, 1964), p. 332.
[19] Weber, *The Theory* . . . , p. 370.
[20] *Ibid.*, p. 371.

government was attained. Another motive for routinization stems from the negative aspects of charisma referred to earlier: it is very risky for a system of authority to have to rely in the long run solely on its continued ability to distribute psychic and material benefits to its followers.

Routinization, according to Weber, leads to the transformation of a charismatic type into one of the other two, legal or traditional. Among others, he specified the conditions under which it was likely to lead to the emergence of a particular subtype of the traditional type, the patrimonial system. The crucial process involved is the *appropriation of offices,* which, he believed, tends to occur

> in all states resulting from conquest which have become rationalized to form permanent structures; *also of parties and other movements which have originally had a purely charismatic character.* With the process of routinization the charismatic group tends to develop into one of the forms of everyday authority, particularly the patrimonial form in its decentralized variant or the bureaucratic. Its original peculiarities are apt to be retained in the charismatic standards of honour attendant on the social status acquired by heredity *or the holding of offices.* This applies to all who participate in the process of appropriation, the chief himself and the members of his staff.[21]

As for the patrimonial system itself, Weber characterized it as follows:

> The object of obedience is the personal authority of the individual which he enjoys by virtue of his traditional status. The organized group exercising authority is, in the simplest case, primarily based on relations of personal loyalty, cultivated through a common process of education. The person exercising authority is not a "superior," but a personal "chief." His administrative staff does not consist primarily of officials, but of personal retainers. Those subject to authority are not "members" of an association, but are either his traditional "comrades" or his "subjects." What determines the relations of the administrative staff to the chief is not the impersonal obligations of office, but personal loyalty to the chief.[22]

Although the presence of a bureaucracy would at first thought appear to be incompatible with the patrimonial system, Weber re-

---

[21] *Ibid.,* pp. 369–70 (italics mine).
[22] *Ibid.,* p. 341.

marked that it would be possible for a patrimonial ruler "in the interest of his own power and financial provision" to develop "a rational system of administration with technically specialized officials" if the following conditions were met: technical training had to be available; there must be an incentive to have such a policy; and finally, it required "the participation of urban communes as a financial support."[23]

We might add that to the extent that these conditions were met, the system would not be resting on traditional legitimacy alone but would be clearly a particular clustering of traditional and bureaucratic traits. When the process of routinization occurs in the second half of the twentieth century, it can naturally be expected to include additional "rational-legal" aspects such as written constitutions and formal electoral procedures. Furthermore, the charismatic aspects themselves need not entirely disappear and a serious attempt may be made to maintain them in order to retain enthusiasm and instill a willingness to sacrifice present satisfactions in order to reap rewards in the future.[24] Hence, we should expect to witness a shift in the mixture of beliefs rather than the total replacement of one particular set by another.

With these qualifications in mind, it can be seen that the West African party-state approximates Weber's patrimonial type in many important respects. The relationships between the individual at the top and his subordinates, as well as between the ruling group and their followers are indeed based on personal loyalty. The conditions under which the patrimonial system can coexist with a bureaucracy are precisely met by the accidental inheritance of both the bureaucracy itself and of the taxation system that makes its survival possible. But the most telling factor is evidence concerning the appropriation of offices. It is indeed striking that the occurrence of this process has been noted by a variety of observers of the African scene, beginning with Frantz Fanon, who in 1961 bitterly charged that the leaders of one-party states had become "chairmen of the board of a society of impatient profiteers.[25] The ruler and his personal entourage, together with a corps of ranking officials and underlings, "satraps" (top-ranking ter-

---

[23]*Ibid.*, pp. 357–58.
[24]For a discussion and extension of Weber's use of "Charisma," see Edward Shils, "Charisma, Order and Status," *American Sociological Review*, XXX, No. 2 (April, 1965), 199–213.
[25]Frantz Fanon, *Les damnés de la terre* (Paris: François Maspero, 1961), especially pp. 124 ff.

ritorial agents) and their blood relations and clients, have begun to constitute a genuine "bureaucratic gentry," a class based not on their relation to property but on their relation to the state apparatus.[26] Since the holding of political office in many poor countries, where there are relatively few opportunities for economic entrepreneurship, is the major source of economic and social status as well, continued political control is necessary, much as Michels suggested that it was necessary for the leaders of labor unions and European socialist parties.[27]

This tendency is reinforced by the pursuit of economic policies which, in the name of socialism or development, have as their major consequence a redistribution of national income to the benefit of the bureaucratic managers of the economy.[28] This also is compatible with Weber's model. In analyzing the relations of traditional authority to the economic order, he indicated that "running through patriarchalism and patrimonialism generally, there is an inherent tendency to substantive regulation of economic activity." Competitive capitalism is usually neither fostered nor tolerated, but "it is possible for patrimonialism to be organized on a monopolistic basis of meeting its needs, partly by profit-making enterprise, partly by fees, partly by taxes."[29] The contemporary African version of this pattern takes the form of a preference for state enterprises, or at least state participation in enterprises; and a preference for large-scale foreign investors operating under something like a licensing system over small-scale autonomous indigenous investors who are much more difficult to control. In this manner, as Weber pointed out, "The immediate effect of charisma in economic as in other connexions is usually strongly revolutionary; indeed often destructive, because it means new modes of orientation. But in case the process of routinization leads in the direction of traditionalism, its ultimate effect may be exactly the reverse."[30] This is clearly what a critic of Guinea had in mind when he concluded a recent study

---

[26] This concept of social stratification is based on Karl A. Wittvogel, *Oriental Despotism* (New Haven: Yale University Press, 1957), pp. 301–68.
[27] Robert Michels, *Political Parties* (Glencoe, Ill.: The Free Press, 1958), especially Chapter IV, "The Need for the Differentiation of the Working Class," pp. 304–11.
[28] Harry Johnson, "A Theoretical Model of Economic Nationalism in New and Developing States," *Political Science Quarterly*, LXXX, No. 2 (June, 1965), 169–85.
[29] Weber, *The Theory* . . . , pp. 357–58.
[30] *Ibid.*

with the suggestion that after an initial revolutionary orientation, the country had now become a bastion of "neo-colonialism."[31]

The resemblance noted earlier between tendencies visible in the West African party-state and historical examples drawn from Europe or elsewhere is thus far more than a fortuitous parallel but indicates that patterns of authority may be genuinely similar. Since the patrimonial system is one of Weber's "traditional" types, however, at first sight this view raises a serious problem: how can one speak of regimes that are still so to speak in their first generation as being based on traditional authority? The problem is much less serious if we do not require as evidence the disappearance of all other forms of legitimacy, but accept as a significant indicator the coming to light of certain attitudes that stress tradition and if we furthermore broaden the latter concept to include not only pre-European Africa, but other references that imply legitimacy based on the notion "this is how things have always been" as well.

Evidence of this sort is not difficult to find. As was already mentioned earlier, Apter, who initially anticipated routinization of charisma into a legal-rational direction in Ghana, has revised his judgment and now strongly suggests on the basis of new evidence the emergence of a kind of "neo-traditionalism." He stated, in the revised edition of his book, "It seems to me that Ghana politics makes little sense unless one appreciates that what has occurred is a new relationship between traditional and secular politics in the *form* of the mobilization system. At the top of this system is a Presidential monarch—a kind of chief."[32] Furthermore, "Substantive integration, such as it is, has been achieved by the ritualization of charisma into a peculiar mixture of socialism and neo-traditionalism. It is a uniquely Ghanaian blend and the new, noncharismatic role at the top is the Presidential monarch, increasingly backed by force."[33] Suggesting that this is a self-conscious effort on the part of the regime, he examined ideological change and concludes:

> One view is that of society as a continuation of the clan and the chief. The position of Nkrumah is that of a chief. The entire society is composed of clans. The local party figures are related to the clans,

---

[31]That is the theme of the bitter attack by B. Ameillon in *La Guinée, bilan d'une indépendence* (Paris: François Maspero, 1964).
[32]Apter, *Ghana in Transition*, p. 331.
[33]*Ibid.*, p. 337.

and thus the web of association between community and chieftaincy is maintained on a national level. The concept of chieftaincy is the essence of the African personality. The leader is duty bound to serve the state because the state is the ensemble of clans, and the leader himself derives from the clans. Hence the principle of legitimacy is a traditional one.[34]

The last sentence exaggerates the situation; in Ghana as elsewhere, several principles of legitimacy coexist, and legal-rational aspects, expressed through both representative institutions and the bureaucracy, are very important as well. Nevertheless, the recent emergence of tradition as a salient principle is very significant. It indicates a shift from legitimacy based on a future-orientation to legitimacy based on past-orientation. Similar observations can be made about the other countries under consideration. Almost everywhere an attempt has been made to relate the present regime to pre-European African states, most obviously in the case of Mali which views itself as having been "reborn" in 1960. Advocates of African socialism everywhere have stressed that their proposed economic policies are anchored on African traditions.[35]

But "tradition," in today's Africa, does not merely refer to pre-European times. Many political institutions created during the colonial period have become, in the eyes of living men, part of the natural order of things: district commissioners, provincial commissioners, *commandants* and governors are offices hallowed by time; the African occupants of these offices derive their authority partly from the fact that they are legitimate successors to the original charismatic founders.

Finally, "tradition" now includes the dominant party's glorious past. Almost every major speech delivered at a party congress or on some other solemn occasion is devoted to a considerable extent not to a discussion of the present but to the recitation of a litany of milestones in the party's history. Even as this chapter was being written, the Ivory Coast government announced the publication of a "history of the party," which turned out to be none other than the reprinting of a three-volume report gathered in 1950 by a committee of the French

---

[34]*Ibid.*, p. 365.
[35]See, for example, the author's analysis of this theme at the 1962 Dakar Conference on African Socialism, in William H. Friedland and Carl G. Rosberg, Jr. (eds.), *African Socialism* (Stanford, Calif.: Stanford University Press, 1964), pp. 122–23.

National Assembly on the origins of the R.D.A. and the troubled times of 1949–1950.[36] In Mali, Modibo Keita's claim to rule is based not only on the fact that he was properly elected, that he bears the name Keita, but also on the fact that he alone is the legitimate successor of the party founder, Mamadou Konaté. In the midst of rapidly changing circumstances, in a society where history remains primarily a matter of verbal record, events that occurred fifteen to twenty years ago can easily become part of a hallowed tradition on which the regime attempts to base its contemporary legitimacy.

The real test of the nature of authority in West Africa, however, can only be provided by a systematic examination of the beliefs of followers. This alone can reveal whether and on what basis they are willing to obey. That this sort of investigation has not yet been carried out illustrates how much we do not yet know and points to some of the tasks that await new waves of political scientists.

THE PERSPECTIVE OF TIME

Much of the discussion about the West African party-state concerns not its present but its future. Many projections, however, rest on an erroneous view of its present characteristics, and it is hoped that the present work will provide a useful corrective. But what of the method of projection itself? On the whole, observers concerned with long-term trends tend to peer into the contemporary party-state and then debate whether they can detect embryonic democracies or embryonic totalitarian systems. This suggests that in borrowing the concept of "development" or "growth" from biology, political science has tended to include the notion that "the adult is 'implicit' in the egg in the sense that one day it will be possible, after determining certain parameters, to read off the constitutional properties of the adult animal from a detailed knowledge of the chemical structure of the egg it arose from."[37]

Is it really useful to view, say, the England of Magna Carta as an embryo of contemporary Great Britain, or the United States of 1789 as an infant who grew into the present giant? To pursue the analogy, it

---

[36] *Fraternité*, August 13, 1965. For the character of this report and its history, see the author's *One-Party Government in the Ivory Coast* (Princeton: Princeton University Press, 1964), p. 111, n. 13.

[37] P. B. Medawar, "Onwards from Spencer," *Encounter*, XXI, No. 3 (September, 1963), 37–38.

might be useful instead to conceive of political systems as they exist at any given time as fairly mature organisms. Long-term changes then appear to be more akin to the biological notion of evolution, *a change from one system to another,* like the evolution of earthworm-making instructions into instructions for making frogs. Although this concept cannot serve as a theoretical guide for the study of political change and development, it can clarify our thinking about change itself. As in biology, "there is no useful sense in which the structure of the mammal is implicit in the structure of a protozoon"—although one can always trace the links in the evolutionary chain *ex post facto*[38]—so we cannot hope to find out, by deciphering the structural code of contemporary political systems, the instructions which will rule one which is to appear in the future.

Instead, we might choose a medium-term view—say, two decades at the most—and then focus on important environmental parameters such as the international system, demography, the economic system, social stratification, about which we can obtain a fair amount of reliable information for this time period, project them into the future, and try to imagine, with the help of evidence drawn from analogous clusterings of variables elsewhere in the political universe (including its extension to include the historical past) what states of the political system would be most compatible with these parametric values, distinguishing with Easton between the levels of "political community," "regime," and "authorities."[39] This approximation might then be modified to take into account the heritage of political culture that is now being created, as well as the more general feedback of the system to its environment, which is but another way of saying that any attempt to understand the evolution of the universe must now take into account the phenomenon of man.[40] To do this systematically is another challenging undertaking for the political science community. Although this task lies beyond the scope of this book, it is nevertheless tempting to make a few suggestions.

A major question concerns, for example, the effects of the international environment on the West African political systems. The situation in this respect is fundamentally different from what it was during the period of state-formation in Europe or from what it is at the

---
[38] *Ibid.*
[39] Easton, pp. 85–86, 116–17.
[40] Pierre Teilhard de Chardin, *The Phenomenon of Man* (New York: Harper and Brothers, 1959).

present time in other underdeveloped regions such as Asia. The West African party-states are not surrounded by powerful neighbors that can absorb or dismember them. They are surrounded mostly by other countries like themselves which also have a limited capability for bringing about fundamental change, although they can contribute to the instability of incumbent authorities by sponsoring opposition groups, etc. Furthermore, as authorities in one country are threatened, the process is likely to have a generalized effect on its neighbors by escalating the cycle of insecurity-repression-subversion-coups. Although the West African party-states could theoretically bring about fundamental changes in their political community through voluntary mergers, such as federations, this is unlikely to happen because the maintenance of the regime and the authorities is closely tied up with the manageability afforded by territorial political control.

The most powerful contemporary political actors may have an interest in influencing particular authorities and even in replacing them with others more amenable to certain policies, and be capable of bringing these changes about if necessary; but on the whole they are not likely to divert their resources in attempts to bring about fundamental changes at the level of the political community or even at the level of the regime. Indeed, the present international political system is most likely to guarantee the survival of the political communities of West Africa, not only by not interfering with them, but by providing tangible reinforcements of their identity through devices such as international organizations in which they have an assigned place, and even by intervening if necessary to maintain their integrity. In short, in the medium term the international political system is likely to effect few changes at the level of the political community or of the regime, but it may contribute to the instability of the authorities.

Turning now to the other social systems within the society, we find that there already exist some important economic differences among the countries in the group. Estimated per capita income in 1961 ranged from about $200 for Ghana, with Senegal and the Ivory Coast not far behind, to about $60 for Guinea and Mali. The absolute size of GNP, which gives us an idea of the total pool of resources available, varied even more, ranging from a high of about $1,375 million for Ghana to a low of about $185 million for Guinea. Other economic indicators confirm this ranking. It is likely that the relatively richer countries in the group will make more progress in economic development than the poorer ones (1) because their present level of achievement already reflects the availability of certain resources; (2) because the relative magnitude of the economy provides at least some opportunities for internal savings and investment by either private entrepreneurs or government; and (3) because external resources (from foreign governments as well as private capitalists) are more likely to flow there than to countries that have no prospects at all for development.

In the poorer countries, unless there are radical changes in the demographic situation, the economic welfare of the bulk of the population will tend to remain at its present level. Since on the whole there has been less exposure to modernity, the population is less likely to undergo what is usually called "the revolution of rising expectations." Nevertheless, since even in poorer countries current policies favor the growth of education, it is likely that there will be a larger group of individuals with higher aspirations, who will be particularly concerned with access to the sole source of social mobility, the bureaucracy. In the immediate future the annual budget, which averages around $50 million in Mali and Guinea, together with some external aid, will enable the party-state to support its bureaucrats, in governmental administrations and by providing a few additional opportunities in state enterprises. But the saturation point is likely to be reached very quickly without an equivalent increase in over-all governmental capability. Hence the economy and the social stratification system are likely to remain compatible with the present regime, a patrimonial system *cum* bureaucracy. Intergenerational tensions, crises of succession, and other difficulties, however, are likely to create instability at the level of the authorities.

In the richer countries the situation is likely to be very different. Without going into details, it is possible to suggest that as some economic development takes place, the society will continue to undergo tangible transformation. These countries are already characterized by the fact that a substantial proportion of the population is involved in growing cash crops for export, such as coffee and cocoa. In the Ivory Coast, this continues to be encouraged; but even in Ghana, in spite of much talk of fundamental change, "socialism" has not yet affected the agricultural sector of the economy in serious fashion. In these countries there is thus already, and it is likely that there will continue to be, an economic as well as a bureaucratic bourgeoisie, with some overlap between the two. With further changes in social communications, the already substantial stratum of "transitionals" will increase at a rapid rate. Although these systems appear to have a greater capability for the distribution of tangible satisfactions to members, an inflationary process of demand-formation is likely to develop. For these same reasons the struggle between central authorities and their subordinates is likely to be more acute. On the whole, all these factors suggest that the stresses at the level of the authorities *and of the regime* are likely to surpass their capacity to adjust.

What will happen to the party-state under these circumstances? In the first place, it is important to note one characteristic of these systems that is seldom discussed, the factor of *size*. As Servoise has suggested, most of these countries can be thought of as "micro-states."[41] Ghana has about seven million inhabitants, and the others are in the three to four million range, but not all of the inhabitants are actually involved in the modern political sector in a substantial way. The total resources secured and redistributed by the party-state, as indicated in annual budgets, bring home even more dramatically the smallness of total political operations even in the richer countries of the group: this ranges from a maximum of about $250 million in Ghana to about $120 to $150 million in Ivory Coast and Senegal. A major consequence of size is that until major transformations in the society occur, politics will remain manageable with the use of existing methods. In addition, even with anticipated serious stresses at the level of the regime, it is difficult to find alternative sources of authority in the society. Many may have the desire not only to upset the incumbent authorities but to remake the regime in their own image, but few have the capability to pursue the latter goal. Military groups exist and can create disturbances—as they have already done in Togo and Dahomey, for example —but they have only a capacity to bring down governments and to apply pressure on authorities, not to effectively remake the polity.[42]

If grave stresses prevail at the level of the authorities and the regime, the political systems of the richer countries in the group are likely to be characterized by periods of substantial disorder which permeate the entire regime, rather than merely causing changes in a par-

---

[41]R. Servoise, "Whither Black Africa?" in B. de Jouvenel (ed.), *Futuribles* (Geneva: Droz, 1963), pp. 262ff.

[42]For the limitations of the military in countries of this type, see Morris Janowitz, *The Military in the Political Development of New Nations* (Chicago: University of Chicago Press, 1964). Although Ghana must now be added to the list, the proposition itself appears to remain valid.

ticular set of rulers. After a time, however, the new regime is likely to resemble its predecessor because of the absence of alternative possibilities. The painful conclusion is thus that we might expect a sort of institutionalized instability, just as in Latin America over many decades the "coup" became an institution. We shall often see dramatic change, but will probably conclude that *plus ça change, plus c'est la même chose.*

CONCLUSIONS

AS THE PRESENT WORK IS BEING COMPLETED ALMOST EXACTLY TEN YEARS after the publication of the first significant book on the subject, David Apter's *The Gold Coast in Transition,* it seems appropriate to discuss by way of conclusion what can and must be done if the next decade of research is to produce as important a contribution as the first to the understanding of politics in Africa.

Although I have attempted to synthesize and to examine in a somewhat critical manner much of what we have learned during the first decade, very little of what has been stated here can be asserted with the degree of certainty that is required in an established area of scholarship. The data are grossly incomplete and the interpretations are tentative; the concepts are often imprecise, they lack theoretical elegance, and they do not easily lend themselves to formulation as hypotheses which can be tested empirically by the more precise methods already elaborated in other spheres of political science. To the extent that these deficiencies are due to the state of our common knowledge of the subject rather than to the author's own limitations, they provide us with a program of research we are unlikely to exhaust in the near future. I hope that some of the suggestions I have put forward will be viewed by others as working hypotheses and that they will be found useful as guides for the allocation of effort to more specific areas of research than the mere accumulation of information about political events and personalities. Meanwhile, a few avenues of exploration seem to be particularly promising.

1. Although an attempt has been made here to reinterpret the emergence of nationalist movements, it is evident that major gaps remain in our basic knowledge of this period. Because of this, as well as because many of the studies of colonialism have been concerned

with policy and political controversy rather than with the understanding of a system of government in operation, it is extremely difficult to reconstruct a reasonable base line from which later changes can be evaluated adequately. A more thorough examination of the period preceding independence would also afford us greater understanding of the development of political groups and cleavages, of their relationship to the non-political environment, and hence, in general, of the characteristic structures and processes which constitute the legacy which the new African states inherited. Whether the history of this period is gathered by political scientists, historians, or members of other academic disciplines matters little; whoever engages in this undertaking must reach beyond events to record social facts. Because of the lack of written materials this must be done to a considerable extent by means of interviews with individuals in Africa and elsewhere who were in their prime twenty or thirty years ago. Before long, memories of this period will be extinguished.[1]

2. Although some attention has been paid to the general orientation of programs of development and to the rhetoric used in speaking about modernization (the nature of "African Socialism" and other approaches), we have barely begun to analyze the "output" of the political system, or at least of the government, by studying programs in action in various spheres. Besides the fields of political economy and of administrative studies, we must also turn our attention to law, a subject which has been almost completely neglected by social scientists, yet is much too important to be left to lawyers alone. It is useful to remember in this connection that many of the original social theories to which contemporary social science owes its conceptualizations of "development" stemmed initially from historical-legal and historical-administrative studies of European political systems.

3. The study of ideology must be broadened to include what has come to be known within the discipline as the study of political culture. It is necessary to acquire greater understanding not only of normative concepts, but also of the cognitive apparatus concerning politics in order eventually to be able to answer the question, how do Africans perceive the political world? Yet even when this is done, most discussions of the subject are limited, as was our own, in two important ways: first, by considering only the uppermost levels at which ideology is formulated; and second, by restricting analyses to

---

[1] See the group of articles on this subject in the *African Studies Bulletin*, September, 1965.

formal communications, usually in European languages. We must study how these concepts are being transmitted by the leaders to intermediate elites and to the population at large. In order to do this, political scientists (either by acquiring the appropriate skills or by collaborating with others) must develop techniques for retrieving information concerning informal political discourse, carried out mainly in African languages.[2] Finally, if we are to make progress in the study of political integration, we must reconstruct not only the explicit ideology of the leaders, but also the "latent" ideology of the population at large, a subject that has only recently begun to draw attention even in apparently well-studied political systems.[3]

4. One of the implications of the view put forward in Chapter V is that in order to obtain a more general understanding of African politics we must examine what occurs at the more intimate and more particular level of the local community. What is involved is less the study of local government (in its institutional sense) than the study of "government locally," or to use another phrase, the study of "micropolitics." It is significant in this respect that the work of political scientists concerned primarily with the United States in this sphere has contributed, along with the study of developing countries itself, to the almost revolutionary change the discipline has undergone in recent years. In the field of African studies proper, the past division of labor between anthropologists and political scientists led the former to concentrate almost exclusively on the traditional political systems, leaving aside (with a few outstanding exceptions) any thought that these systems have been involved for half a century or so in a larger territorial system.[4] Political scientists, on the other hand, have tended to devote almost their entire effort to the study of the center, with the consequences discussed in earlier chapters. Now, however, this dichotomy can be overcome by a change in the approaches of both disciplines and, it is hoped, by explicit collaboration between them in sharing theoretical insights and in rationalizing the organization of field research.

---

[2] The value of such studies is well demonstrated by W. Whiteley, "Political Concepts and Connotations," in Kenneth Kirkwood (ed.), *St. Anthony Papers No. 10* ("African Affairs No. 1," London: Chatto and Windus, 1961), pp. 7–22.

[3] For the relevance of this type of study, see Robert Lane, *Political Ideology* (New York: The Free Press of Glencoe, 1962).

[4] Two outstanding exceptions are M. G. Smith, *Government in Zazzau* (London: Oxford University Press, 1960), and Lloyd Fallers, *The King's Men* (London: Oxford University Press, 1964).

5. With a slight shift of emphasis, much of what was said in (4) above also applies to the question of the relationship between tradition and modernity in contemporary African states. In exploring this relationship, it is difficult to find solid ground between the extreme constituted by the uncritical acceptance of the principle *post hoc ergo propter hoc,* which leads some scholars to find amidst the many diverse aspects of tradition in a particular country some element that seems to "explain" contemporary behavior, and the other extreme of almost total neglect of the past. The consideration of traditions in Africa is complicated by the fact that to any one contemporary territory, there usually correspond several traditional societies; hence, one must consider not only the traditions of each but also the interplay between them. A second important consideration is that as of now, "tradition" in Africa includes the colonial experience.

6. The study of the West African party-state, as well as of African politics generally, must be more comparative than it has been hitherto. This does not necessarily mean that we must abandon the fruitful tradition of single-country monographs or that all efforts must be guided by a particular theoretical framework. My own inclinations are at least implicit in the present work: I believe that a promising approach consists of comparisons at a middling level of generalization between units that are not extremely diverse, such as contemporary African states themselves, or between them and historical states (in Europe and elsewhere) in which somewhat similar conditions prevailed. What matters more than the choice of a particular strategy, however, is the mood that prevails, the contribution of individual studies to the growth of a "comparative persuasion" which parallels and is complementary to the "behavioral persuasion" of which Dahl has spoken.[5]

Viewed in this way, the study of African politics becomes merely *the study of politics in Africa.* Hence, although these studies require that the researcher acquire special skills and a general know-how concerning the continent, they require even more the maintenance of strong ties with the remainder of the discipline and with the other social sciences. The study of politics in Africa thus ultimately derives its justification much less from the importance of the continent from the point of view of contemporary international politics—a notion

---

[5] Robert Dahl, "The Behavioral Approach," *American Political Science Review,* LV, No. 4 (December, 1961), 763–79.

which I believe to be incorrect—than it does from the contributions it can make to the more general understanding of human experience.

* * *

Many Africans now question the legitimacy of critical examinations of their regimes of the type undertaken in this book. They view the endeavors in which political scientists normally engage as subtle manifestations of the spirit which in the past led white men to assume colonial burdens, because they believe that even a relatively objective approach relies on extraneous criteria and hence implies somehow that non-Africans know what is best for Africa. Paradoxically, even sympathetic observers find themselves in a position similar to that of the regime's internal critics: if they persist in trying to understand political processes when adequate information is denied them, they become vulnerable to the charge of spying and of reaching erroneous conclusions based on incomplete data. Under such circumstances, almost any empirical study takes on the air of an exposé because it clashes with officially approved accounts of events and processes. When this is done by scholars to whom Africans have generously extended hospitality and precious time it amounts to sheer betrayal in the eyes of the Africans.

All of this applies even more forcefully to any attempts by scholars to evaluate African regimes according to the standards of political philosophy. Some observers, out of genuine consideration for the feelings of their African friends, have chosen to remain silent on this score. Others have gone so far as to try to demonstrate that what is must be, that it is the best possible solution under the circumstances, and in particular that in spite of appearances to the contrary the West African party-state has the right to claim for itself the label "democratic." By taking this position, scholars are rendering a grave disservice to political science because the loose application of important concepts reduces their usefulness and dilutes judgment to the point of banality. What they are doing to Africa is even more serious, and has been stated forcefully by W. Arthur Lewis. In a recent article significantly titled "Beyond African Dictatorship," he concludes, speaking of democracy:

> The system still has powerful adherents in the area, who have looked to their fellow democrats outside at least for spiritual com-

fort. They have looked in vain. Western democrats have abandoned the African; even longstanding friends of Africa hesitate to speak out for fear of offending those now in power. As for our political scientists, they fall over themselves to demonstrate that democracy is suitable only for Europeans and North Americans, and in the sacred name of "charisma," "modernisation," and "national unity," call upon us to admire any demagogue who, aided by a loud voice and a bunch of hooligans, captures the state and suppresses his rivals.[6]

It is not to earn the dubious satisfaction of being able to demonstrate that dark-skinned men necessarily err and are incapable of ruling themselves in a reasonable way that we must persist in our inquiries, but rather because to the contrary, we hold them to be men like ourselves. To suggest that the standards we apply to evaluate our own behavior are not appropriate to judge theirs is a form of condescending paternalism hidden beneath a liberal veneer, not very different from the notion that there must be separate standards for civilized men and for barbarians. Hence, we not only have the right to judge, but it is our duty as intellectuals concerned with the fate of men in Africa to do so. Furthermore, it is on the basis of this common humanity that we must also claim the right to study that which is to be evaluated and criticized in the best possible manner. Incidentally it is possible that the understanding obtained through such studies will be of use to Africans themselves much as the study and the critical evaluation of our own regimes, in spite of occasional objections from our fellow-countrymen, is ultimately helpful to our decision-makers who, like their African counterparts, are too closely involved in the political process to be able to view it with detachment and in perspective.

In asserting the right and the duty of foreign students of African politics to observe, evaluate, and criticize, I do not mean to suggest that there is no possibility of perfecting concepts and methods. Although I fully subscribe to the general principle contained in the quotation from Arthur Lewis, I am less sure about the applicability of the concept "democracy" to the evaluation of African regimes. Although Africans themselves, by adopting a populist rhetoric and the formal trappings of democracy, seem to invite the imposition of the democratic template over the West African party-state, when this is done little more can be said than that it does not fit. Going beyond

---

[6] W. Arthur Lewis, "Beyond African Dictatorship," *Encounter*, XXV, No. 2 (August, 1965), 18.

CONCLUSIONS

this, and keeping in mind the consequences of the sectoral view of the political system advanced in Chapter V, it is possible to suggest that "democracy" and its polar opposite in the contemporary political jargon, "totalitarianism," are largely irrelevant terms because they are designed to deal with relatively highly integrated political systems. There is a suggestive parallel in economics: "capitalism" and "socialism," however useful they may be to characterize certain types of economic systems, lose much of their heuristic value when applied to underdeveloped economies in which from one-third to one-half of the GNP is produced in a residual traditional sector. To return to the political sphere, it is self-evident that "totalitarianism" is by definition incompatible with the notion of a large sector of political activity that remains beyond the reach of the regime. But what of "democracy"?

Although this concept usually includes the notion of a limited regime, the limitations are significant only because they are self-imposed, voluntary, and do not stem merely from a lack of capability. On the positive side, "democracy" in its contemporary sense is usually assumed to be meaningful only if it applies, at least in principle, to the right of all to participate in decision-making. Hence even at best, if political competition and the rule of law were institutionalized in the modern sector of the West African party-state, it would be misleading to speak of "democracy" as long as entirely different norms prevail in the residual sector.

The concept of democracy *could,* of course, be applied to the modern political sector exclusively, ignoring its relationship to the society at large. It could even be argued that there is an outstanding precedent for this, since Aristotle saw democracy "wherever the free-born are sovereign," and presumably would have included in this category pre-Civil War United States or the Union of South Africa of a few decades ago, when freedom still prevailed in the European community, but coexisted with a hierarchical relationship between this sector and the remainder of the political system. If we wish to follow this precedent in unmodified form today, we must bear at least the onus of a philosophic justification for such a serious departure from contemporary norms.

That may not be necessary. The interpretation put forward in this book suggests that the West African regimes are populist and nationalist avatars of what used to be called "oligarchies" or "despotic states," and were considered *sui generis* before these political terms had acquired inescapable pejorative connotations. Since political philosophers of the past had much to say about such regimes, their conceptual apparatus might be very helpful in studying the present and in providing criteria of philosophic understanding which transcend contemporary contingencies. Their successors who are concerned with the study of new states, as they ought to be if their claim to universal relevance is to be meaningful, can provide the necessary guidance by recasting their approach. Perhaps when they do so they will experience the same sense of discovery and of renewal as students of comparative politics did when they ventured to explore the new states.

* * *

My own views on this subject can be stated succinctly. That genuine democracy in one of its many forms is a suitable regime for men in Africa as elsewhere can be stated without a doubt; that the rulers of most West African states as well as the bulk of the intellectuals deserve to be blamed for not having tried very hard to bring about such a regime is also quite clear. On the other hand, I doubt very much, for reasons discussed earlier, whether, even if the best men available devoted all their energies to the task, democracy would flourish in West Africa in the near future. That does not mean, however, that Africans cannot stem present trends toward ever-greater authoritarianism and even to a certain extent reverse the tide.

The crux of the problem lies in the view that authoritarian measures are necessary to maintain order and to bring about modernization in the political, the economic, and other spheres. I disagree with this view on two grounds. First of all, although authoritarianism has been historically successful elsewhere in achieving such goals, the costs incurred are extremely great, and if Africans wish to live up to their claim that they have a valuable contribution to make to mankind, they owe it to themselves as well as to the rest of us not to sacrifice their humanism for the sake of other values which they are the first to deplore as the tragic flaw of European civilization. In the second place, practically speaking, it is unlikely that an imitative authoritarianism would be as successful in Africa as it was in the original from which it is copied, not because African tyrants are necessarily less skillful than European ones, but rather because other conditions that contributed to the success of authoritarian rulers, such as the scale of the political community, its physical resources, and the cultural predispositions of the population, are simply not met. Hence, efforts in this direction are doomed to failure.

CONCLUSIONS

Since these efforts are made in keeping with the directives of the ideological map that is common to most leaders, it is the map itself that must be altered. This map contains misleading normative and cognitive components. African leaders have adopted unrealistic goals: in the economic field they are willing to listen only to advisers who promise that by allocating their scarce resources in some magic way, they will rapidly overcome poverty; in the political sphere, they suffer from their own mistaken beliefs that they will earn the respect of the remainder of mankind only if they can suddenly emerge as powerful states which superficially resemble their erstwhile European masters or other members of the international political community. These unrealistic goals are accompanied by what we have characterized as a mechanical view of appropriate means; the paraphernalia of the state is conceived as a set of levers with which to apply direct pressure on the political community in order to bring about achievement of these stated goals.

The consequences are as we have discussed them in earlier chapters. Since the huge effort expended far exceeds the capabilities of the system and the results are far short of anticipated goals, the entire process exposes the rulers to painful frustrations and in turn to a generalized loss of temper and a ritualization of authority which leads them to treat their countrymen much as old-fashioned schoolteachers treat children.

Paradoxically, in spite of the failure to bring about fundamental change, most of the West-African party-states have been able to cope fairly well so far with a variety of stresses. They have adequately managed their apparatus of government and in some cases have even been able to expand it somewhat beyond what it was during the colonial period, despite the loss of expatriate personnel. But it is almost impossible to attribute these successes, and even the few economic gains, to the most recent transformations of the regime in a more authoritarian direction. On the contrary, it is much more likely that these successes are due in part to the persistence of bureaucratic institutions inherited from the colonial period, but mainly to the continued exercise by the rulers of the political skills that enabled them to construct and manage the nationalist movements a decade or so ago. In other words, whatever success does occur stems from the fact that the regime has retained some of the characteristics it had acquired at an earlier period, when we suggested it could be described as a political machine.

Since it is primarily because the goals of the organization had been substantially redefined at the time of independence that unsuccessful attempts to change the entire regime were launched, the adoption of a set of goals that would resemble those that prevailed earlier would probably relieve much of the strain. The result would be that the structure and the norms characteristic of the West African party-state would resemble the sorts of political arrangements that are still visible in industrialized countries below the national level, within some federal unit or at the municipal level, and which were more common before those countries became fully industrialized and modernized.

Although the political machine is not usually associated with the exercise of sovereignty, this is not a very serious objection to its suitability for Africa, since we have already seen that the international political system tends to guarantee the maintenance of the political communities that now exist. The national interest of African states does not require the exercise of military power or the maintenance of a garrison state, but rather constant bargaining, a task for which machine politicians are eminently suited. A second objection may be that machines lack dignity and tend to be corrupt. But what is usually called corruption in this context can be viewed, under certain circumstances, as a fairly rational distributive system which is based on other than rational-legal norms, and hence is better adapted than bureaucracy to societies of this type. Furthermore, it is likely that corruption is associated with a whole set of factors, and hence that it will prevail even if the rulers attempt to construct an authoritarian regime based on revolutionary puritanism.

The machine is particularly suitable to govern relatively small political communities in transition, and provides both flexibility and stability. By shunning serious commitment to a very demanding ideology, the machine maintains solidarity among its members by appealing to their self-interest while allowing for the play of factions and for recurrent reconciliation. It can easily provide for the formal and informal representation of a multitude of relatively modern and not-so-modern groups in the society, including those based on common origin and those based on explicit economic or political interests. Intelligent machines can even coexist with and benefit from reform-minded groups led by highly educated men by setting aside given sectors (such as certain specialized parts of the bureaucracy) in which these groups can carry out their own activities relatively undisturbed. While retaining a great deal of flexibility, the machine can sustain a powerful central authority which will cope with certain community-wide problems if the boss is an enlightened one. Throughout, the machine remains genuinely popular. It does not require that its leaders rise far above the mass or cut off all contact with it. Furthermore, because its inner workings are very informal, patterns of behavior and norms which might otherwise be dismissed as "unmodern" are quite acceptable; individuals who do not possess rare legal or bureaucratic skills and who would otherwise be set aside can still participate in politics and make a significant contribution to government. Finally, a machine can coexist with a variety of economic arrangements, ranging from private local entrepreneurships to non-resident large-scale enterprises, and public corporations. Although it tends to redistribute income to the benefit of its own members, this membership basis tends to be broader than it would be in more hierarchical systems.

Such a regime is not streamlined; it lacks a sense of glory and does not insure that there will be an immediate and revolutionary change in the human condition. But it is known to have operated successfully in West Africa. It is not genuinely democratic but it tends to avoid senseless cruelty. Beyond this, it might help relieve the heavy burdens of imitation and self-doubt with which Africans have been saddled too long and might enable them to regain confidence in their ability to rule themselves. That, ultimately, is the only soil in which democracy has been known to grow.

INDEX

Abidjan, 69, 118
Aboisso, 69
academic freedom, 79. *See also* universities
accountability, 66
Accra, 68, 117, 119
Adamafio, Tawia, 96
Adande, Alexandre, 49
administration. *See* bureaucracy
agitation, as technique, 13
Agni, 69, 77, 116
agricultural groups, 72
Akan, 91, 110
Akim Abuakwa, 118
Alassane Haidara. *See* Haidara, Mohammed Alassane
Alexander, A. S., Jr., 108
allocation of values, 131. *See also* authority, political system
anarchy, 11
Andrain, Charles, 60
Ansprenger, Franz, 29
anti-intellectualism, 121. *See also* intellectuals, universities
appropriation of offices, 140
Apter, David E., 3, 4, 22, 34, 39, 48, 64, 70, 78, 123, 136, 138, 151
armies. *See* coups d'état, military in politics
Ashanti, 14–15, 20, 24–26, 38, 67, 73, 76–77, 117
assassination, 76. *See also* coups d'état
assemblies. *See* national assemblies
Austin, Dennis, 13, 20, 58, 81
authoritarianism, 2, 56, 66, 72, 79, 87–90, 111, 134, 155–58. *See also* totalitarianism
authority, 3, 17, 107, 123, 128, 134, 137–39, 142. *See also* legitimacy
autocracy. *See* authoritarianism

Baako, Koffi, 58
BAG. *See Bloc Africain de Guinée*
Bamako, 31
Bambara, 69, 76
bandwagon effect, 19, 22–25
Baoule, 26, 110
basic committees, 104
Bayer, Ronald, 112
BDS. *See Bloc Démocratique Sénégalais*
Beaujeu-Garnier, J., 29
beliefs, 50, 60, 145. *See also* ideology
Benjamin, Ernst, 98
Berg, Elliot J., 72

Bété, 69
Bingerville, 69
Birmingham, Walter, 20
Blanchet, André, 38
Blocs Africain de Guinée, 30, 46
Bloc Démocratique Sénégalais, 16, 53. *See also Union Progressiste Sénégalaise*
Bloc Populaire Sénégalais, 26, 34
Bohannan, Paul, 76, 132
Botsio, Kojo, 96
Boucle du Niger, 31
Bowen, Elenore Smith, 76
Bowman, Larry, 73
Boyon, Jacques, 23
BPS. *See Bloc Populaire Sénégalais*
Bretton, Henry, 4, 23, 56
brigades de vigilance, 104
British Labour party, 22
Buell, Raymond L., 133
Buganda, 136
Bureau Politique, 104
bureaucracy, 41, 71, 99, 102, 106–7, 114–19, 124, 139–42, 148, 159. *See also* government
Butler, Jeffrey, 72

cabalistic thought, 64, 92
cadre parties. *See* patron parties
Campbell, A., 20
Cape Coast, 69
capitalism, 63, 142
Casamance, 26
categoric groups, 71
centralization, 107, 125, 135
CGT. *See Confédération Générale du Travail,* 43
charisma, 3, 17, 137–39, 142. *See also* authority, legitimacy
Charles, Bernard, 29, 102
chef de canton. See chiefs
chiefs, 12, 21, 26–28, 30–31, 71, 106–7, 114–20, 143. *See also* traditional system
Christianity, 139
civil service, 41, 71, 99, 102, 106–7, 119–21, 124. *See also* bureaucracy
clans, in Senegal, 16, 26
classes, 51–52, 71. *See also* cleavages
cleavages, 12, 21, 45–47, 51–55, 67, 71–75, 92. *See also* conflict, opposition
clerks, 120

163

INDEX

coercion, 66, 77–78, 82–90, 126. *See also* authoritarianism
Coffie-Crabbe, H., 96
cognitive apparatus, 152. *See also* ideology
Coleman, James Samuel, 75
Coleman, James Smoot, 21, 61, 70, 101, 123, 127
colonial systems, 17, 25, 28, 41, 116
Colony (Ghana), 14–15, 24
communes, 118. *See also* local government, urban politics
communications, 48, 54, 66, 105, 114, 131, 148
communism, 22, 64. *See also* Marxism, totalitarianism
Conakry, 69, 76, 103
Conférence Nationale des Cadres, 105, 113
conflict, 64, 75, 87, 122: intergenerational, 12, 67, 73–74, 125, 148. *See also* cleavages, ethnicity, opposition
Congo, 2, 6, 136
Congress for Cultural Freedom, 48
Conseil Economique et Social, 113
Constitutions, 34, 66, 106–8, 141
consultation, 66, 114
Convention People's Party, 3–4, 13–22, 34, 38, 56, 75, 81, 95–98, 112, 138. *See also* Ghana, Kwame Nkrumah
Converse, P., 20
cooperatives, 96
co-optation, as technique, 66
corporations, 113
corruption, 119–21, 160
Coser, Lewis, 75
Coulibaly, Ouezzin, 32
counter-revolutionaries, 62
coups d'état, 6, 11, 71, 76, 84, 91, 98, 109, 149–50. *See also* insecurity
courts. *See* judicial process
Cowan, L. Gray, 29, 102, 105
CPP. *See* Convention People's Party
cultural strain, 39

Dahl, Robert, 154
Dahomey, 49, 52, 149
Dakar, 26–27, 68, 119
Dalton, George, 132
danger, perceptions of, 42. *See also* insecurity
Danquah, J. B., 67, 84, 118
death penalty, 84–86. *See also* coercion
decolonization, 38. *See also* colonial systems
de Gaulle, Charles, 38, 43, 50. *See also* Referendum of 1958

Delval, J., 31
demands, 126
democracy, 2–5, 49, 53–55, 64, 82, 112, 119, 145, 155–58
deportation, 82. *See also* coercion
despotism, 111, 157. *See also* authoritarianism
detention of opponents, 78. *See also* coercion
Deutsch, Karl, 130
development, 145
Dia, Mamadou, 85
Diallo, Saifoulaye, 30
dictatorship, 2, 56, 155. *See also* authoritarianism
differentiation. *See* cleavages
disorder, 4–5
Djoloff, 27
Dogon, 69
dominant parties, emergence of, 9
Doob, Leonard, 39
Du Bois, Victor, 102
duties, 104
Duverger, Maurice, 10

Easton, David, 67, 128, 138, 146
Ebrié, 68
economics, 63, 72, 132, 147. *See also* socialism
education, 71, 148. *See also* universities
Edusei, Krobo, 96
Eisenstadt, S. N., 74
elections, 13, 19, 141; in Ghana, 15, 20, 24, 76, 81–88, 118; in Guinea, 29–30, 80; in Ivory Coast, 15, 25, 80; in Mali, 31–33, 80; in Senegal, 16, 80; under one-party state, 66, 75, 79–82
elite, 36, 39
elite parties. *See* patron parties
Emerson, Rupert, 13
environment, of political system, 67
Estates-General of the Ivory Coast, 113
ethnicity, political aspects of, 22, 26, 30–31, 35, 40–41, 45–46, 50, 53, 68–70, 82, 97–99, 103. *See also specific tribes and peoples*
Ewe, 70, 91
executive, national, 19, 66, 107–15, 136, 142. *See also* authority, government
exile, as technique, 66. *See also* coercion

factionalism, 135
Fallers, Lloyd, 136, 153
family, 74, 103. *See also* kinship
Fanon, Frantz, 141

INDEX

Fanti, 69
Farmers Council, 96
Fascist parties, 23
fear, of rulers, 76. *See also* insecurity
federalism, 62, 70, 107
feedback, 146
field administration, 114. *See also* bureaucracy, government
Fily Dabo Sissoko. *See* Sissoko, Fily Dabo
Foltz, William J., 53, 62, 101
fragmentation, process of, 19–26
France, 13, 25, 28, 50
freedom of the press, 79. *See also* communications
French Community, 38, 42. *See also* de Gaulle, Charles
French Sudan. *See* Mali
French West Africa, 26, 28, 41. *See also* French-speaking Africa
French-speaking Africa, 13, 26, 28, 35, 41, 53, 78–79, 107, 110, 120. *See also under specific countries*
Friedland, William H., 63
Fulani, 31, 116
Futa-Djalon, 28
Futa Toro, 27

Ga, 68, 91, 97, 117
Geertz, Clifford, 22, 39–42, 64
general will, 62
generations. *See* conflict, students
Ghana, 1–2, 7, 13, 17–18, 21–24, 35–38, 41–42, 48, 56, 61, 67–73, 77–84, 89, 91, 95, 106, 109–13, 117, 120, 124, 136–38, 143, 147–49. *See also* Convention People's Party, elections, Kwame Nkrumah
Gold Coast. *See* Ghana
government, 52, 93, 125, 126, 142. *See also* bureaucracy
Grand Bassam, 69
Great Britain, 13, 50
grievances, under colonial systems, 12
Groupe d'Etudes Communistes, 28, 30
guided democracy, 64. *See also* democracy
Guinea, 7, 18, 27–30, 38, 43, 54, 61, 77–80, 85, 91, 101–8, 112–15, 123, 133, 147. *See also* elections, *Parti Démocratique de Guinée*, Sékou Touré

habeas corpus, in Ghana, 83. *See also* judicial process
Haidara, Mohammed Alassane, 31
Haines, C. Grove, 21
Hanna, William John, 37

head of state. *See* executive
Hodgkin, Thomas, 9, 37
Houphouet-Boigny, Félix, 15–17, 38, 42, 54, 110. *See also* Ivory Coast, *Parti Démocratique de Côte d'Ivoire*

identity, national. *See* national integration
ideology, 5–7, 37–65, 79, 91–93, 125, 145, 152, 159; Ghana, 56–59; Guinea, 43–46; Ivory Coast, 54–55; Mali, 50–53; Senegal, 46–50. *See also* democracy, Marxism, nationalism, socialism
imperialism, 58, 64
independent churches, 12. *See also* religion
indirect rule, 116. *See also* colonial systems
insecurity, of rulers, 4, 11, 39–43, 59, 76, 92
instability, 11. *See also coups d'état*, insecurity
institutions: transfer of, 4, 41; creation of, 41, 66. *See also* government, political parties
instruments of rule, 61, 93–126. *See also* government, political parties
integration. *See* national integration
intellectuals, 44, 48, 60, 74, 79, 98, 121, 156. *See also* conflict, intergenerational
interests, 52
intergenerational conflict. *See* conflict, intergenerational
international system, 41, 129, 146
Islam, 26, 28, 46, 69, 139
Ivory Coast, 7, 15–17, 21, 25, 38, 41, 51–54, 61, 69, 76–80, 85–86, 89–91, 99–101, 112–15, 124, 144, 147–48. *See also* elections, Houphouet-Boigny, *Parti Démocratique de Côte d'Ivoire*

Jacobins, 62, 71
Jahoda, Gustav, 18, 20
Janowitz, Morris, 149
Johnson, Harry, 142
journalists, 48. *See also* communications
JRDACI. *See Parti Démocratique de Côte d'Ivoire*
judicial process, 66, 78, 82–87, 107

Kaplan, Morton A., 129
Kayes, 69–70
Keita, as lineage, 110, 136
Keita, Madeira, 28, 52–53
Keita, Modibo, 31, 104, 136, 145
Kennedy, John F., 76
kinship, 22, 74, 103
Konaté, Mamadou, 30, 32, 145

165

INDEX

Kornhauser, William, 14
Kraus, Jon M., 88, 113
Krobo, Edusei. *See* Edusei, Krobo
Kumasi, 119. *See also* Ashanti

labor unions, 28–30, 60, 72, 96, 102, 104, 142
Lamine-Gueye, 68
Lane, Robert, 59, 153
language, 46
Latin America, 150
Lebou, 26, 68
legal institutions, 106, 152. *See also* judicial process
legal-rational legitimacy. *See* legitimacy
legitimacy, 3, 17, 47, 137, 144, 154–55. *See also* authority
Lerner, Daniel, 12, 131
Lewis, W. Arthur, 155
liberalism, 68
Lingère, 27
local government, 106–7, 114–19, 153. *See also* chiefs, urban politics
loyalty, 66, 84, 115
Lumumba, Patrice, 50, 76

machine, as a political model, 18, 22, 123, 159
Mackintosh, J., 21
Madeira Keita. *See* Keita, Madeira
magic, 76
Maiga, as lineage, 31
majority rule, 55
Mali, Empire of, 31
Mali, Federation of, 50
Mali, Republic of, 7, 27, 30–33, 54, 61, 69, 80, 85, 103–6, 108, 112–15, 123, 133, 136, 145–47. *See also* Keita, Modibo; Union Soudanaise
Malinké, 27–31, 76
Mamadou Konaté, *see* Konaté, Mamadou
Mannoni, O., 18
Marxism, 22, 45, 52, 60, 64, 94, 102, 137
mass movements, 9–16, 19, 28, 33–35, 151. *See also* political parties
mechanical thought, 64
medieval Europe, 136
messianic cults, 12, 139. *See also* religion
Michels, Robert, 142
micro-politics, 153
Milcent, Ernest, 29
militants, 126
military in politics, 11, 98, 149. *See also* coups d'état
Miller, W., 20

Minianka, 69
mobilization, 25, 34, 126–27, 131
Mockey, Jean-Baptiste, 99
modernization, 40, 123, 127, 131
Modibo, Keita. *See* Keita, Modibo
monarchies, 56, 140–44
monistic model, 60
monocephalism, 109, 111, 125
Morgenthau, Ruth Schachter, 3, 9, 18, 32, 61
Mossi, 116
movements. *See* mass movements
municipal government, 107. *See also* local governments, urban politics
Muslims. *See* Islam

NASSO. *See* National Association of Socialist Students' Organization
nation-building. *See* national integration
National Assemblies, 11–12
National Association of Socialist Students' Organization, 95
national integration, 40–45, 51–55, 60, 93, 123, 131
National Liberation Movement, 20, 25, 76
nationalism, 1, 37, 41, 46, 57
nationalist movements, 11, 33, 35, 151. *See also* mass movements
neo-colonialism, 64
Neumann, Sigmund, 2
newspapers, 54, 105. *See also* communications
Niger, 136
Nigeria, 2, 21, 48, 70, 133, 136
Nkrumah, Kwame, 6, 12, 17, 23, 38, 57, 63, 76, 96, 98, 118, 120, 136, 143. *See also* Convention People's Party, Ghana
Nkrumahism, 59
NLM. *See* National Liberation Movement
no-party state, 127
normative concepts, 152
Nyerere, Julius, 48
N'Zérékoré, 29

oligarchies, 157
Olympio, Sylvanus, 76
oneness, as concept, 71, 93. *See also* unity
one-party democracy. *See* democracy, ideology
one-party ideology. *See* ideology
one-party state. *See* West African party-state *and under specific countries*
opposition, 5, 26, 46–48, 50–51, 67–68, 66–92, 135. *See also* cleavages, coercion, elections

INDEX

order, concern with, 40, 90, 126, 139
Ouezzin Coulibaly. *See* Coulibaly, Ouezzin

pagans, 69. *See also* religion
Pan-Africanism, 62
Parliament. *See* national assemblies
parliamentary system, 108
Parti Démocratique de Côte d'Ivoire, 14, 16–17, 26, 34, 38, 54–55, 99–101. *See also* Houphouet-Boigny, Ivory Coast
Parti Démocratique de Guinée, 28–30, 34, 43, 46, 101–3
Parti de la Fédération Africaine, 50–51
Parti Soudanais Progressiste, 30–33
parties, 9–10, 12–16, 19, 23, 28, 34–35, 46, 93, 99, 101–3, 121, 125, 144. *See also under specific organizations*
party-state. *See* West African party-state
patrimonial system, 140–44. *See also* traditional system
patron parties, 10, 28, 35. *See also* parties
PDCI. *See* Parti Démocratique de Côte d'Ivoire
PDG. *See* Parti Démocratique de Guinée
PFA. *See* Parti de la Fédération Africaine
Pinto, I., 49
planning, 63–64, 71
plots. *See* coups d'état
pluralistic model, 60
political cleavages. *See* cleavages
political community 46, 146, 160
political communications. *See* communications
political conflict. *See* conflict
political culture, 29, 146, 152
political institutions. *See* government, parties
political integration. *See* national integration
political participation, 19, 26, 31, 67, 131
political philosophy, 155
political recruitment, 74, 79, 87, 113
political religion, as concept, 64
political socialization. *See* political recruitment
political system, 6, 128–34
political thought. *See* ideology
pragmatic-pluralist regimes, 7, 122
presidential monarch, 136, 143. *See also* executive
presidential system. *See* executive
press, 48, 54, 105. *See also* communications
preventive detention, 67, 78, 83. *See* coercion
primary groups. *See* ethnicity, kinship

primordial solidarities. *See* ethnicity, kinship
Protestantism, 110. *See also* religion
PSP. *See* Parti Soudanais Progressiste
psychological pressures. *See* insecurity
punishment. *See* coercion
Pye, L., 73, 90

racism, 53. *See also* ethnicity
Rassemblement Démocratique Africain, 12, 16, 18, 28, 29, 31, 37, 138, 145. *See also* Parti Démocratique de Côte d'Ivoire; Parti Démocratique de Guinée; Union Soudanaise
rationality, 63, 123. *See also* order, planning
reconciliation, 87, 127
recruitment. *See* political recruitment
Referendum of 1958, 38, 43, 79. *See also* elections
refugees, 77
regime, 66, 75, 146
regionalism, 52
religion, 12, 46, 53, 69, 110, 136
representative councils, 19, 66
repression. *See* coercion
republicanism, 68, 109. *See also* presidential authority
revolution, 41, 57
revolutionary-centralizing regimes, 7, 123. *See also* mobilization
ritual, 89
Robinson, Kenneth, 25, 34
Rosberg, Carl G., Jr., 63, 101, 123, 127
routinization. *See* charisma
rule of law, 5, 78, 82. *See also* democracy

Saifoulaye Diallo. *See* Diallo, Saifoulaye
Saint Louis, 27, 69
Sarakollé, 31
Schachter, Ruth. *See* Morgenthau, Ruth Schachter
Schumpeter, Joseph, 2
Ségou, 76
Senegal, 7, 16, 21, 26, 34, 50–54, 60, 67, 77, 80, 85, 101, 107–8, 124, 147. *See also* Senghor, L. S., *Union Progressiste Sénégalaise*
Senghor, Léopold Sedar, 16, 50–51, 84. *See also* Senegal
Senufo, 69
separatism, 71
Servoise, René, 149
Shils, Edward, 5, 141
Sigmund, Paul E., 48
Sikasso, 31

Simmel, Georg, 75
Siné-Saloum, 27
single-party systems. *See* West African party-state
Sissoko, Fily Dabo, 30
Smith, M. G., 153
Snowiss, Leo, 73
social communications. *See* communications
social stratification, 148. *See also* classes, cleavages
socialism, 63, 142, 148. *See also* economics
Socialist parties, 27–29, 46
Soussou, 69, 76
sovereignty, 160
Soviet Union, as model, 64, 124. *See also* totalitarianism
state apparatus, 52, 92, 126, 142. *See also* bureaucracy, government
Stokes, D., 20
strain. *See* insecurity
strikes, 76. *See also* labor unions
structure, of parties, 5–6, 10, 123, 128
students, 67, 77, 122. *See also* conflict, intergenerational
Sudan, French. *See* Mali
support, 15
Sutton, Francis X., 63
symbols, 64, 107, 109, 110

Talmon, J. L., 62
Tanzania, 135
technocrats, 125
Timbuktu, 31, 85
Togo, 70, 76–77, 149
totalitarianism, 5, 64, 88, 124, 145, 157. *See also* authoritarianism, mobilization
Touré, as lineage, 31, 110
Touré, Sékou, 18, 28, 32, 43–44, 60. *See also* Guinea, *Parti Démocratique de Guinée*
towns. *See* urban politics
trade unions. *See* labor unions
Trades Union Congress, 96
traditional chiefs. *See* chiefs
traditional system, 21, 26, 30, 57, 61, 70–71, 103, 133, 137, 140–42, 154. *See also* chiefs, legitimacy
traditionals, as category, 22, 131
transitionals, as category, 12, 14, 22, 131, 148
Trans-Volta-Togoland, 24

treason, 84. *See also* loyalty
tribalism. *See* ethnicity
trusteeship, 70
Tuareg, 85
Tukulor, 27
turnout. *See* political participation
tutelary democracy. *See* democracy
tyrannies, 56. *See also* authoritarianism

Uganda, 70, 133, 135
unanimity, 66–91, 112, 131. *See also* unity
unions. *See* labor unions
United Gold Coast Convention, 67
United States, Congress, 77, 112
universities, 79, 98, 121. *See also* conflict, intergenerational; intellectuals
Union Progressiste Sénégalaise, 16, 53, 68, 81. *See also* Senegal; Senghor, Léopold
Union Soudanaise, 28, 31–34, 52–53, 103–6, 136. *See also* Keita, Modibo; Mali
unity, 37, 45–46, 60–62, 71, 79, 87, 93, 112, 131. *See also* national integration
Upper Volta, 52, 116
UPS. *See Union Progressiste Sénégalaise*
urban politics, 15, 68, 107, 118. *See also* local government
US. *See Union Soudanaise*

vanguard activists, 95
Vansina, Jan, 136
Vignaud, M., 25
violence, 75–76. *See also coups d'état*
voluntary associations, 53, 66, 82. *See also* labor unions, students

Wallerstein, Immanuel, 11, 44
Weber, Max, 136–37
Weiner, Myron, 93
Welbeck, N. A., 96
West African party-state, 6–7, 11, 35–37, 51–52, 82, 127–28, 134, 137, 141
Whitely, W., 153
witchcraft, 76
Wittvogel, Karl A., 142
Wolof-Sérère, 27
World War II, effects of, 12
Wright, Richard, 23

Yacé, Phillipe, 92, 99
youth organizations, 74, 96, 100, 104. *See also* conflict, intergenerational; students

PRINTED IN U.S.A.